To Chuck -

Great friend
and colleague ...
Richest blessings
as you GO
making "worshiping
disciples on mission"!

Mark Powers

Going Full Circle

Going Full Circle

Worship that Moves Us to Discipleship and Missions

Mark C. Powers

RESOURCE *Publications* • Eugene, Oregon

GOING FULL CIRCLE
Worship that Moves Us to Discipleship and Missions

Resource Publications
An Imprint of Wipf and Stock Publishers
199 W. 8th Ave., Suite 3
Eugene, OR 97401
www.wipfandstock.com

ISBN 13: 978-1-62032-994-8
Manufactured in the U.S.A.

This book is dedicated to worship leaders everywhere.
May God use it to move you and your teams full circle
to become worshiping disciples on mission.

Contents

Diagrams

Foreword

Why Do You Go to Church?

By Charles Billingsley

Why do you go to church? Why are you a part of a church? What's the point of this whole thing, anyway?

I was brought up in the church. In fact, I was a Southern Baptist nine months before I was born. All I have ever known is church life—not only its culture, politics, quirkiness, and ugliness, but also its beauty and the heart of its mission.

I have lived long enough and been in enough behind-closed-door meetings to know that what happens on the platform Sunday morning does not always represent what is happening Monday through Saturday. Whether it be problems related to relationships, money, numerical growth, spiritual growth, or whatever, it seems all local church bodies go through a myriad of issues on almost a weekly basis.

Part of this is due, of course, to the fact that we, as believers, have a great adversary in Satan, and he does not want the church to succeed in any way, shape, or form. He likes nothing more than to fill our sanctuaries and the lives of Christ followers with innumerable distractions. He uses everything from busy personal schedules at work to squealing monitors on a stage to try to distract us from our worship experience and ultimately our true calling as believers.

But I believe the rest of it can be attributed to an overall spirit of indifference. As I travel the country, and having been in almost 2,000 churches now, it is rare that I encounter a body of believers whose focus is outward to the community. Rather, the focus tends to lean inward toward ourselves.

In so doing, we have missed our true calling as the children of the living, redeeming, almighty God.

Our true calling is really quite simple. We find it first in Deuteronomy 6:5. Then we see it again in Matthew 22:37 and Mark 12:30. Our true calling is to "love the Lord our God with all our hearts." As all Sunday school children are taught, this is the greatest commandment. This is truly what it means to worship God, simply to love him with a lifestyle that honors him and blesses him. To do so in every aspect of our lives is to live the greatest commandment. However, Jesus added another great commandment to this first one. He also said to "love your neighbor as yourself" (Mark 12:31). This is called the second greatest commandment. There is no hint of indifference in either of these commandments. So, if we are going to love God with our whole heart, soul, mind, and strength, then the natural outflow of that will be that we love others as he loved us.

But this is where the trouble begins. Granted, self-focus is usually not the mindset of a new Christian. In fact, most new adult Christians have just been rescued out of a lifestyle of sin that had held them in bondage and misery, so they are free for the first time and can't wait to share the good news of what Jesus has done in their lives. No, this indifferent mindset doesn't set in until we have been in church a little while. It takes a few years, but once the initial emotional charge has simmered, all this new convert has to do is settle into a life of weekly church-going. It is here that he or she can develop a new set of friends, a new system of values, a new repertoire of songs, and even a new list of complaints. Oh don't get me wrong, they have been changed by the Savior. But the church has a way of dulling our senses to the culture around us and even has a way of taking us completely out of it. And that's bad.

This new Christian can easily merge into the massive flow of fellow believers and sing his heart out on Sunday mornings, give 10 percent or more in the offering, and "amen" every good point the pastor makes, while at the same time becoming completely disengaged from that ugly sinful culture outside the walls of his own church building. So, instead of going out into the world as Jesus calls us to do, we develop a proclivity to just sing louder and give more from the inside. It's just easier that way. Plus, the sacrifice is way less risky.

We have created our own little world within the world. It's a world where only "Christian" things are true, where everyone lives happily ever after, and most importantly, where we can be safe from the other world--that big, crazy, godless world out there. As a result we have Christian music, Christian coffee, Christian bookstores, Christian schools, Christian clothes, Christian jewelry, Christian radio, Christian TV, Christian movies, entire Christian industries. If we are not careful, we can exist entirely in our own subculture. I am just as guilty of this as anyone.

Don't misunderstand me. I am a worship leader. I want my congregation to sing loudly their praises to God. I want a body of believers who tithe and live upright, holy, and godly lives. And, of course, God inhabits this worship. He wants it too. But we must also never forget that the God we worship is also the Savior who told us to "go and make disciples!"

Jesus said we are to be in the world, but not of it. What world is he talking about? This one! The world of the Bible is the same one we live in today. And, as Chuck Colson said, "The way we see the world can change the world."

The book you are about to read is all about this subject. How can we effectively move from being complacent churchgoers to dynamic disciple-makers? How can we transform the church from an institution back to a mighty movement? Can God still use us? Does he still want to? Can we develop a healthy Christian worldview that is grounded in the passion of the great commandment yet culturally relevant enough to carry out the Great Commission? You will find those answers and more in this wonderful book by my friend, Mark Powers. I pray it enlightens you, convicts you, and becomes a catalyst for change in the body of Christ.

Charles Billingsley
Worship leader, Thomas Road Baptist Church, Lynchburg, Va.
Artist-in-Residence, Liberty University, Lynchburg, Va.

Acknowledgments

I LIVED DAILY IN humble amazement at God's provision as I wrote this book. Every step of the way, he was there providing each piece of the full circle puzzle at the right time in the right way just as I was ready for it. All glory to him!

To my editors: Allen Hendricks, content editor and worship guru; Curt Watke, content editor and missions guru; and Margaret Colson, copy editor par excellence.

To my family: Jean and Wildred Powers, my mother and father, who taught me to think outside the church box; my wife, Kay, for common-sense editing and constant love and encouragement; my son, Jeremy, the best theologian/philosopher I know personally; my daughter, Lauren, the best musician I know personally (who also loves circles).

To other wonderful friends who read parts of the manuscript and advised: Lee McDerment, Kevin Batson, David Parks, Monty Hale, Mike Glenn, Reggie McNeal, Charles Billingsley, Charles Roberts. To Henry Deneen, my childhood friend, now President of Greater Europe Mission, for a missional vision imparted over lunch in Columbia in 2010. To Dr. Jim Austin, Executive Director, SC Baptist Convention, for your encouragement and support.

And to my fellow state Baptist convention music leaders who kept telling me to write the book. Let's start a nationwide music-arts mission movement together!

At the conclusion of each chapter, sections entitled "Return to the Cross" are meditations on historic hymns of our faith in the public domain. Copyright restrictions made it difficult to use more modern hymns and choruses. Be inspired by these classic hymns and know that I have no prejudice against songs of today.

1

The Wrong Track

It's a recurring dream of mine—a nightmare, really. We are all together on this train. It's called the Church Train.[1] We've traveled the same track for many years. Those who grew up on the Church Train cannot comprehend any other track. After all, we've been on this track as long as we can remember. Traveling happily along in the club car—the church club car—we are very comfortable with the way we do things. The pastor and staff serve as stewards, keeping us inspired and happy, attending to our needs with great dedication as we travel this track. On occasion our train pulls into a station. Those of us on the Church Train eagerly invite those standing on the platform to join us. Don't they see that our train is a happy place to be? We can't fathom why anyone would refuse a ride in our club car. We've done our best to decorate in a way that would be inviting to those outside. Yet, most of them refuse to join us on our train. We don't really understand why.

Lately, some riders on our train have upset us. They look down the track and say we're headed for disaster. We haven't paid them much attention. They say there is a landslide ahead. We are headed for a plunge into destruction, they claim. How strange to hear those on our own train say such things. Surely God would not allow such a thing to happen to the Church Train. Some keep whispering about how we need to build an alternate track that will take us to a different destination. The radicals say we ought to get off the Church Train and move among the people. But, as hard as I try, I can't get off the train. It's a recurring dream of mine—a nightmare, really. We are all together on this train. It's called the Church Train . . .

> As he approached Jerusalem and saw the city, he wept over it and said, "If you, even you had only known on this day what would bring you peace—but now it is hidden from your eyes.

1. The Church Train metaphor was first developed by Curt Watke, director, Intercultural Institute for Contextual Ministry, www.iicm.net.

> The days will come upon you when your enemies will build an embankment against you and encircle you and hem you in on every side. They will dash you to the ground, you and the children within your walls. They will not leave one stone on another, because you did not recognize the time of God's coming to you." Luke 19:41–44, NIV

During Jesus' entry into Jerusalem, he looked into the near future and foresaw the Temple under siege by outside forces. He prophesied that this institution of Jewish religion would fall to destruction. Just a few years from that day the prophecy was fulfilled.

Today, the institutional church is under siege. Just as in Jesus' day, church people like you and me are blind to the part we are playing in the process of its downfall. If we stay on this track we are headed for a landslide.

Have you seen the latest statistics about the evangelical church? It's quite possible that you have not paid attention and are still assuming that all is well in our churches. We who have lived most of our lives inside the walls of churches have a tendency to live in our own world, don't we? But if you are paying attention at all, you have an inkling that things are not like they used to be in church. Attendance is down, budgets are tight, and friends are being released from staff positions. Statistics point to the church's diminishing influence in society, and we are being laughed at in the secular media. Our Church Train surely is headed down the wrong track.

According to Thom Rainer, president and CEO of LifeWay Christian Resources, in the United States 65 percent of the Builder Generation (born prior to 1946) is Christian, while just 35 percent of the Boomers (born 1946 to 1964) and only 15 percent of the Busters (born 1965 to 1983) claim a relationship with Jesus. The numbers for Generation X and Y (born since 1984) continue this dramatic downward spiral. In Great Britain and Europe, there are places where only one percent of the population is in church on any given Sunday. Even in the Bible Belt of America, church attendance is losing ground quickly. In a 2011 study, the Barna group discovered that 41 percent of all Americans are unable to identify any individual who they consider to be an influential Christian.[2]

Those raised in church can hardly comprehend these facts. We have lived in the comfort and confines of the church club car all our lives. So

2. "Top Trends of 2011: Changing Role of Christianity." No pages. Online: http://www.barna.org/faith-spirituality/543-top-trends-of-2011-changing-role-of-christianity.

our worldview is very narrow when we look out the window of the Church Train. But the bad news doesn't end there.

Church growth experts say that as many as 30 to 40 percent of our existing churches could close their doors within the next 25 years. This statistic is not limited to traditional churches only. Churches started just 10 to 20 years ago with contemporary worship styles are just as liable to fall into the church club car trap. Does it alarm you that 25 years from now, one out of every three churches in your community may be closed? Had you realized that the church today is going downhill that fast? Would it really matter to your community if your own church closed its doors today? Would your neighbors miss your church if it no longer existed? Those are tough questions, but we must ask.

This decline is not just limited to those outside the church. Among church members, too, the statistics are telling. According to the 2011 Barna study quoted above, most Americans—roughly four out of five—considered themselves to be Christians. For this group of professing Christians, the 20-year period from 1991 to 2011 was a time of substantial change in their religious behavior:

- The largest change in belief was the ten-point decline in those who firmly believe that the Bible is accurate in all the principles it teaches. Only 43 percent of self-identified Christians had such a strong belief in the Bible in 2011.
- Whereas 30 percent of the self-identified Christians volunteered at a church during a typical week in 1991, that figure declined to 22 percent in 2011. It's no wonder that churches are struggling to provide the number of programs and ministries that were once a staple of their existence.
- Not only has volunteerism declined in church, but also attendance at church services declined among self-identified Christians by nine percentage points across those two decades. These days less than half of those calling themselves Christian (47% in 2011) could be found in church during a typical week.
- Even more telling, less than one out of five (18%) of this group attended Sunday School or a small group Bible study during a typical week by 2011.

> The hand of the LORD was upon me, and he brought me out by the Spirit and set me in the middle of a valley; it was full of bones. He led me back and forth among them, and I saw a great many bones on the floor of this valley, bones that were very dry. He asked me, "Son of man, can these bones live?" I said, "O Sovereign Lord, you alone know." So I prophesied as He commanded me and breath entered them; they came to life and stood up on their feet—a vast army. Ezekiel 37:1–3,10, NIV

Please understand what I am not saying. The body of Christ is not doomed. The kingdom of God and of his Christ shall reign forever and ever! I am not saying we should be the voice of doom. A sign in a national tool distributor shows these words super-imposed over photos of all varieties of tools: "The Bad News: Our World is Falling Apart. The Good News: Our World is Falling Apart." To us who have trouble using a hammer, the knowledge that the world is falling apart is bad news. But to those who earn a living by fixing things, a world falling apart means they will never run out of work. Our Almighty God has the power to fix this world. He uses our brokenness to heal, help, and move us to his purposes. The Church is his body, and he is the healer of broken bones. Ezekiel experienced firsthand God's power to put us back together when the body of believers seemed dead and disjointed. So we need to remind ourselves every day that, though institutional churches are in trouble, God's church for whom Jesus died will endure into eternity. May we never stop praying for revival in our land.

But until revival comes, worship leaders must find the courage to look beyond our job security as stewards of the Church Train and see reality. It requires real courage. It also requires faith in God and in the people of God. Most of all, it requires that we know that God will build his church when we follow his blueprint. Jesus said the people of Jerusalem could not know the way to peace because it was hidden from their eyes. Oftentimes, the people who are most involved in an institution are the last ones to see its decline. We are like homeowners on TV renovation shows. When outsiders tour the home and make negative comments about the design and décor of an older home, the homeowners get quite defensive and angry. The longer we live in one place, the less we truly see what is going on around us. We get blinded by our presuppositions, stuck in deceptive mindsets, held captive by our refusal to see objectively. God must take the dry bones of familiarity and breathe in new life. Only then can we become the vast army he is calling us to be.

Do you have the courage to see what is really happening in our churches? Will you ask God to open your eyes and see the truth? That's not easy. The process is not for the faint-hearted or weak. You will have to confront your own shortcomings and misguided mindsets in the same way that I have had to confront my own. We are people who truly love our churches and our love reflects God's love for his church. So I ask you right now for the privilege of leading you on this journey of confronting the old ways of thinking that have led us to decline. I beg your permission to let me guide you lovingly and carefully in the thought process through which God has led me. Will you allow me to speak heart to heart with you from God's Holy Word? Let's ask God to guide us in this journey to rediscover his blueprint for the church. Come alive, dry bones, and go forth as a mighty army—the people of God!

Return to the Cross

"When I Survey the Wondrous Cross" is widely regarded as the most popular Christian hymn in the world. Isaac Watts, the English hymn writer, wrote this great hymn of our faith in 1707.

When I survey the wondrous cross,
On which the Prince of glory died,
My richest gain I count but loss,
And pour contempt on all my pride.
Forbid it, Lord, that I should boast,
Save in the death of Christ, my God;
All the vain things that charm me most,
I sacrifice them to His blood.[3]

Oh, Lord, when I see what you have done for me by sending Jesus to die on the cross for my sin, I am overwhelmed. Nothing that I personally could ever achieve could count more than the gift of your Son. Nothing in which I could ever take pride could equal your love for me. Yet Lord, I have taken the cross for granted. Christ's gift of his blood and his body too easily becomes old news to those of us in church. I keep asking this question. It haunts me as I stand to sing another hymn on another Sunday in another worship service across these long years of church attendance. Would you, Almighty God, the creator of the universe, send your Son to die for me

3. Watts, "When I Survey the Wondrous Cross," Public Domain.

just so we can have a somewhat inspiring and mildly entertaining worship service each week? Is that why you sacrificed your very own Son to a violent death on a cruel cross? There must be more! Show us, O Lord, what more there is to worship. Heal the blindness that comes from being too familiar with church, and worship, and you.

Questions for Thought and Discussion

Do the statistics quoted in this chapter shock you? Why or why not?

How do you see these declining statistics reflected in the churches around you? How much of this decline can you attribute to the Church Train mentality?

What are some effects that the Church Train mentality has in your own life? In the church you attend?

How does the confession of Isaac Watts in "When I Survey the Wondrous Cross" reflect the change of direction needed in churches today? What are the essential things that this great hymn calls us to experience spiritually?

Pray a prayer that reflects your need to experience those essential spiritual attitudes.

2

We Do Church Right!

> In the year that King Uzziah died, I saw the Lord seated on a throne, high and exalted, and the train of his robe filled the temple. Above him were seraphim, each with six wings: With two wings they covered their faces, with two they covered their feet, and with two they were flying. And they were calling to one another: Holy, holy, holy is the Lord Almighty; the whole earth is full of his glory." At the sound of their voices the doorposts and thresholds shook and the temple was filled with smoke.
>
> "Woe to me!" I cried. "I am ruined! For I am a man of unclean lips, and I live among a people of unclean lips, and my eyes have seen the King, the LORD Almighty." Isaiah 6:1-5, NIV

I SPENT 30 YEARS of my life and ministry in the institutional church serving the Church Train. As a worship and music pastor, I poured my life into providing the best Sunday worship experiences that I could lead our teams to produce. No, the doorposts didn't shake, there was no smoke, and the Lord never appeared visibly, but worship was quite good, if I do so say myself. Many times as I walked off the platform after Sunday worship I would think with satisfaction (paraphrasing a famous chicken restaurant slogan), "We do church right." The choir and orchestra had sung and played their best; the praise team had lifted us up with excellence; the pastor had preached an inspiring sermon; and the congregation had worshiped with full participation. My calling as a worship leader had once again been fulfilled, and I could look to the next Sunday and plan for another high time of worship. And that was the total sum of who and what I was as a professional minister of music/worship leader, to my way of thinking at that time.

But then my life took a dramatic turn. After 28 years in local church ministry, God called me into denominational work to equip and train churches for worship and music on the state level. I began to hear and see the statistics that I quoted in chapter one. I had never realized how church decline was sweeping the modern evangelical church. "How could this be?" I thought. Surely these numbers must be wrong. We may not be doing great, but I certainly thought that we were holding our own. After all, we do church right. But the facts were correct, and the decline was inescapable. And the more I visited churches and studied the findings, the more I could see it for myself. I became discouraged. I was hurt. I was horrified that the beloved institution I had served for 28 years was rushing toward a fall that could wreck it. While my heart recoiled in frustration, my mind immediately began to question and look for answers. If the way we are doing church is leading us to a steep decline, what can we do about it? Where did we get off on this track headed in the wrong direction? How can we get on the right track? But my next thought hurt even more deeply. What have I personally been doing wrong all these years?

Soon afterward, as I was experiencing a powerful worship moment in my home church, a question came to me from God: "Where in the Bible does it say we will win the world by getting the world into the church?"

"But God," I argued, "Getting people to come to church is the bedrock of all we've been doing in church all these years. We're trying our best to offer great experiences that draw people into the church building so that they can hear the gospel and hopefully accept Jesus as Savior and Lord. This is what it's all about, right? And furthermore, we will send missionaries to start churches in foreign lands so that our missionaries will win the world by getting those people into those churches. And we will start churches in our town across the tracks from us, so that their pastors will win them by getting those people into their churches. That's the way it works in your kingdom, right God?"

But the question came again: "Where in the Bible does it say we will win the world by getting the world into the church?"

> Then one of the seraphs flew to me with a live coal in his hand, which he had taken with tongs from the altar. With it

> he touched my mouth and said, "See, this has touched your lips; your guilt is taken away and your sin atoned for." Then I heard the voice of the Lord saying, "Whom shall I send? And who will go for us?" And I said, "Here am I. Send me!" Isaiah 6:6–7, NIV

The prophet Isaiah also heard a question from God. One day while serving in the temple, Isaiah was overwhelmed by a vision of God in all his power and might. Confronted by the glory of God, Isaiah confessed his sin, and God forgave him. Before we can answer God's most penetrating questions, he wants to do business with our hearts. Before God can use us we must be broken of our ego and self-centeredness. When Isaiah saw God's incredible glory, he was awestruck. But he didn't just stand there thrilled at the awesome display of God's glory as great entertainment. No, Isaiah was immediately overwhelmed by his own inadequacy and sinfulness. I imagine that he fell down prostrate before Almighty God, his voice trembling, tears in his eyes. "Woe to me, I am ruined. For I am a man of unclean lips . . ." Brokenness is an appointment with God that you can't make, because God makes it with you. If the Lord God can't work with me, then he will work without me. His mission to redeem the world to himself will be accomplished with or without us. If we allow our heart and ego to be broken, God can use us in his redemption plan for the world. The way up is down; we become instruments of God's grace when we fall on our face before his presence.

God's call to us, like his call to Isaiah, begins with brokenness. The call of God always starts there, of course. But God's call also includes the call to discipleship and mission. God commissioned Isaiah to go to his people and proclaim his prophetic Word. Isaiah might have devalued this vision as simply an emotional reaction to grief over the death of his king. But God made the vision concrete when he said "Go." Isaiah could have ignored God's call to mission, fulfilling his duties to the Church Train in the operation of temple life.

But God said, "Go."

The message that God told Isaiah to preach was not an easy one. It was a promise of captivity because God's people had abandoned what he told them to be and to do. They had hardened their hearts toward God, and God said Isaiah's prophetic message would only harden their hearts further, certainly not an inviting job to be called to accomplish. Isaiah probably wanted to run and hide from such a confrontational message.

But God said, "Go."

Isaiah responded, "Here am I, send me."

Institutional churches are driven by a methodology called attractional worship. It begins with the mistaken notion that our primary strategy to win the world should be getting people into church. Attractional thinking drives the church to present the very best services, events, and activities to attract non-believers. But, non-believers are not capable of worshiping God because they are spiritually dead. The Holy Spirit must bring them to life before they can worship the God of life. In contrast, biblical worship empowers Christians to fall deeply in love with God, submit to his transforming process as a disciple, and go on mission to their community. God did not design worship to create spectators, nor to build the institutional church by keeping members happy, nor to win the world by attracting people into our churches. Worship in spirit and truth is focused on God alone and moves his children to grow up as disciples and go out as missionaries. Why? God's primary strategy to win the world is to get his church into the world, not the world into churches.

Let me be clear. Jesus did attract large crowds of people throughout his ministry. Our worship should be attractive, too. But Jesus continually called his followers out of the crowd to deeper discipleship and mission. Our Lord did not build his kingdom on crowds; he built his kingdom on disciples. If we celebrate the number coming in our front door but fail to grow them as disciples and send them back out that door, we have missed the gospel and created "club car keepers".

Are we growing true disciples in our worship ministries? Are our churches making disciples who are on daily mission with God in their family, school, workplace, and community? Sadly, the statistics say we are not. This failing is clearly not determined by worship style either. Contemporary worship leaders sometimes think they have achieved the highest of heights with cutting-edge music and technology and their ability to draw a crowd. Meanwhile, our traditional musicians hold onto their performance standards like a child's security blanket. But neither our contemporary church-starts nor our old-line established churches are showing much long-term success beyond satisfying the needs of the church club car, regardless of what form it takes. Clearly worship style is no guarantee of effective disciple-making. Regardless of what we call it, our scorecard for doing church right in the institutional church has usually been: counting monetary gifts, counting the number of people in attendance, and measuring the size of our buildings. Yes, these are important in gauging the effectiveness of our churches. But the real shortcoming in this gauge is that it doesn't measure true discipleship or our heart for the mission of God. How in the world can we measure that?

The real issue is our heart. Regardless of our worship style, we are very likely to repeat these shortcomings for generations to come if we do not grasp the change of heart needed to grow disciples who make disciples. What a terrible tragedy it would be for us to pass down to another generation the misunderstanding of God's call to be worshiping disciples on mission.

> He said, "Go and tell this people: 'Be ever hearing, but never understanding; be ever seeing, but never perceiving.'"
> Isaiah 6:9, NIV

Another issue to consider in studying Isaiah 6 is that God called Isaiah to his own people. In verse nine, God told Isaiah, "Go and tell this people." He was to announce God's warning to those who lived all around him. Obviously, there are those like Jonah in the Old Testament and Paul in the New Testament whom God called to live and preach in foreign lands. However, most of the prophets and apostles God called were sent to their own people. What can we learn from this? Christ's Great Commission to us includes the call to go both to our own community and to the people groups beyond our own. In obedience, many evangelical churches take mission trips to other states and other countries. This is good. God calls us to go to other people groups. But too often the participants return from such a trip only to go right back inside their churches and forget those all around them. If a mission trip away from home ignites us to become missionaries to our home community, then it is very profitable. But if missions to those far away is simply a checkmark on our church list before we go back to business as usual maintaining our club car, then we have fallen far short.

Here is how we know we are falling short in God's call to make disciples who make disciples:

- Polls report that, on average, only three out of every 100 church members in the U.S. ever share their faith. Only one of those shares their faith regularly.
- The latest statistics point to the fact that North America is the only continent in the world where Christianity is in decline as a percentage of the population. According to the Association of Religion Data

Archives (www.thearda.com), the percentage of total population claiming adherence to a Christian religious group in the United States declined from 50.2 percent in 2000 to 48.8 percent in 2010.

- The Pew Forum on Religion & Public Life reported in October 2012 that the number of religiously unaffiliated Americans rose from 15 percent to 20 percent in only five years. This increase is most prominent among the young, with one third of those under age 30 claiming no religious affiliation.
- North America has the third largest block of unbelievers in the world only after China and India.

Those of us who love the church should be shocked. These facts tell us that North America is no longer the main missionary-sending continent in the world. Instead, North America has become the main mission field in today's world. Nations once considered by American Christians to be primary mission fields are now sending missionaries to us. All around us are those who have no knowledge of relationship with God through Jesus. Like Isaiah, we are surrounded by those who have hardened their hearts to God and his love. And that hardness is not limited to those outside the church. As in Isaiah's day, the people of God have hardened their hearts to all God has called us to be and to do. Which of these is more difficult: To get people outside the church interested in Jesus, or to get people inside the church interested in those outside to share Jesus with them? Indeed, most of us in the church are not sure if we even know people who are not Christian. And beyond that, we are not so sure we want to know them. We are much more comfortable staying in the church club car, making occasional forays outside to issue impersonal invitations to those along the tracks before we scurry back into the safety of the Church Train.

So where in the Bible does it say we will win the world by getting the world into the church? It doesn't. The Bible never says that. It says we will win the world by sending the church into the world! It says we are to be salt and light to those around us. When we spend all of our extra time at church doing churchy things with churchy people, should we be surprised that our churches are in decline?

I have asked this question in every situation where I have been given opportunity. But there are other questions that beg to be asked, as well. "Do you think you will achieve church unity by having all your people sit in the same room for an hour every week?" No, church unity is achieved by joining God on his mission and moving your people toward that mission every day in every way.

"Will we build the church by offering a worship style that keeps our members happy but never deepens their discipleship or calls them to join God on mission?" Ultimately, true worship always leads to true discipleship and the real call to be on mission, just as it did for Isaiah. But there is no particular worship style that will guarantee that your people will become true disciples or join God on mission.

There are traditional churches proud to uphold their ritual heritage and preach social gospel, yet blind to the real needs of those around them. There are ethnic churches trumpeting their stylistic variety, yet deaf to the need to grow true disciples serving in their own community. There are mega-churches offering exciting blended worship, yet primarily focused on building their own mega-institution. There are booming contemporary churches seeing large numbers respond to the gospel only to have them become no more than a spectator congregation each Sunday.

When our God, high and lifted up in all his glory and holiness, bursts into our lives, our only acceptable response is surrender. When we are staring at God face-to-face, worship style becomes secondary. Repentance will mean everything, and "Yes" will be our best response.

If we love the church, and I do, we must find our prophetic voice and sound the alarm. Shallow self-serving worship will create shallow self-serving Christians secure in the comfort of the church club car headed for a crash. When we make worship nothing more than meeting our felt needs, it's too easy to experience heavenly worship while continuing to live like hell. If we don't wake up to the voice of God, we are doomed to repeat the institutional pattern for generations to come, regardless of how exciting or moving our worship is to us right now. Join me in this journey to rediscover real worship that will ignite you to discipleship and mission. Milburn Price and Gary Furr, in *Dialogue of Worship: Creating Space for Revelation and Response,* wrote: "The application of the structure of Isaiah's experience . . . provides a model for corporate reenactments of the kind of divine-human encounters essential for maturing spirituality."[1]

That day in worship when I saw the Lord high and lifted up, God asked me a question that started my journey to a new level of spiritual thinking. "Where in the Bible does it say we will win the world by getting them into church?"

1. Price and Furr, *Dialogue of Worship: Creating Space for Revelation and Response*, 3.

Can you hear the voice of the Lord saying to you, "Whom shall I send? And who will go for us?" How will you answer God's question?

Return to the Cross

Were you there when they crucified my Lord?
Were you there when they crucified my Lord?
Oh! Sometimes it causes me to tremble, tremble, tremble.
Were you there, when they crucified my Lord?[2]

Have you trembled lately? Have you seen God so high and lifted up in power that it caused you to fall down and lay helpless on the ground trembling? Have you been so awestruck in his presence that you could not speak or run or hide, that all you could do is stand there and tremble? Why not?

Were you there when they laid Him in the tomb?
Were you there when they laid Him in the tomb?
Oh! Sometimes it causes me to tremble, tremble, tremble.
Were you there when they laid Him in the tomb?

Have you died lately? Have you seen Jesus so high and lifted up on the cross that it caused you to fall down crying, lying broken on the ground trembling? Have you been so awestruck in the presence of his sacrificial death for you that you could not speak or run or hide; that all you could do is stand there and wish it was you who was dying? Why not?

Were you there when He rose up from the grave?
Were you there when He rose up from the grave?
Oh! Sometimes it causes me to tremble, tremble, tremble.
Were you there when He rose up from the grave?

Have you lived lately? Have you been starving to know the presence of God? Have you seen Jesus gesture for you to follow? Have you heard his voice calling you to go? Why not?

2. Work, Jr. and Work, "Were You There," Public Domain.

Questions for Thought and Discussion

What things give you the most pride about your church? Are those elements of your church life fulfilling God's mission to redeem the world or simply building the institutional church? How?

Recall a time in your life when you "saw God high and lifted up" and how you reacted. Recall a different time in your life when God allowed you to be broken. How have these two life experiences impacted your life since then?

Write a definition of discipleship that expresses what you think it is at present. Write a definition of missions that expresses your understanding now. Keep these two definitions for comparison to those you will write later in this study.

If you were to hear the voice of the Lord saying to you, "Whom shall I send? And who will go for us?" how will you answer the question right now?

3

How Did We Get Here?

> The wisdom of the prudent is to give thought
> to their ways, but the folly of fools is deception.
> Proverbs 14:8, NIV

I WAS THE GUEST leader at a small church for morning worship recently. I led the worship songs, directed the choir, and encouraged the worship leaders and members to make worship their lifestyle. The accompaniment to the worship songs was the pianist and a lone guitarist sitting beside the unused electronic organ. As I led the songs, I noticed that the pianist was struggling, but the guitarist was fairly adept at accompanying. His guitar amp was sitting on top of the organ facing the congregation, but I could hardly hear him. After the service, I complimented the guitarist and suggested that he turn up the volume so as to be a more effective accompanist. I also wanted to suggest that he place his guitar amp behind him so that he could hear himself better. As we talked I noticed that he appeared to be hard of hearing. After a few words he reached to his ears and pulled out a wad of tissue from each ear.

Grinning at him, I asked: "Why did you have those in your ears?"

"Well," he said very seriously, "our pianist went to hear the Gaither Vocal Band and she told me they had these things in their ears to help them hear, so I started putting these wads of tissue in my ears each Sunday, and it really helps!"

Obviously, the electronic in-ear monitors the professionals use are not the same as wads of tissue stuck in your ears. I tried to explain this to him but soon gave up.

Like the fellow with the tissue in his ears, we don't know what we don't know. If I asked you, "What is the most important thing right now that you do not know," of course, you would say, "I don't know." Why? Because we don't know what we don't know.

If someone we respect tells us something, then we assume it is true. We have no real reason to doubt because it seems right to our way of thinking. Once we try it, and it seems to work, we continue to do it. We may grow up hearing a half-truth all our lives, but because everyone is telling us and it seems to be working, we believe it. So we sometimes foolishly live in deception because we just don't know what we don't know. Someone has said, "One thing we learn from history is that we seldom learn from history."

So if we as worshipers and worship leaders really want to be a part of the solution, we must find out what we don't know. Do you want to help prevent our Church Train from the landslide looming in the distance? Will you accept as truth the statistics of church decline and resolve to do something about it? It demands a long, hard look at ourselves on three levels.

First, we must discover how we got here. Knowing the track we are locked into will help us know how to build an alternate track to our original destination.

Second, we must rediscover the essence of true worship to see how it can power our train back to our original destination.

Third, we must take a hard look at our worship, comparing it to God's standard to identify idolatry hidden within.

Without this honest appraisal, our Church Train will continue its mad rush toward the crash. Are you courageous enough to join me in this journey for the next three chapters?

> Everyone was filled with awe at the many wonders and signs performed by the apostles. All the believers were together and had everything in common. They sold property and possessions to give to anyone who had need. Every day they continued to meet together in the temple courts. They broke bread in their homes and ate together with glad and sincere hearts, praising God and enjoying the favor of all the people. And the Lord added to their number daily those who were being saved. Acts 2:43–47, NIV

How does the institutional church of today compare to the early Christian church?

Characteristic	Early Church	Institutional Church
Location	Homes	Nice Buildings
Size/Dynamic	Small/Interaction	Large/Observation
Support	Meet each others' needs	See the ministerial staff
Pastor's Role	Lead disciple-making/ Teach	Preach good sermons/CEO
Leader's Task	Grow disciples	Direct programs and events
Laity's Role	Make disciples	Attend/Serve the institution
Key Words	Disciples who make disciples	Come have your needs met
Teaching	Embody Christ	Teach doctrinal belief
Commitment	Grow God's kingdom	Grow my church
Staff Development	Raise up from within	Hire outside professional
Accountability	Everyone's role	No one's role

You can see from this chart that the early church was very missional and not very institutional in comparison to churches today. Yet within two or three centuries, institutionalism crept into the early church too. Before long, Christianity began to be sidetracked by "church-ianity."[1]

The process goes something like this: God moves among people. They open their hearts to the changing power of Christ and accept him as Savior and Lord. They join or start a group of believers in a home or public venue. They are eager to worship Jesus, learn of him, and share him with their friends. This is church the way God intended it to be.

This energetic cycle is an exciting thing to be a part of as God manifests his kingdom work in the hearts and actions of his people. But eventually something happens to break this cycle. Slowly, and often without anyone really noticing, the process turns inward. Because we are sinful, we are self-centered. Self-centered people tend to create self-serving organizations. The intention of the church goes from the cycle of worship-discipleship-mission to self-sustaining-and-maintaining. It's an ongoing tendency that we must battle constantly.

1. The term, "church-ianity" is attributed to Curt Watke, director, Intercultural Institute for Contextual Ministry, www.iicm.net.

It's like the rescue society in New England. They were formed to build and run a lighthouse to steer ships away from the rocks. Long hours of training in rescue techniques followed. Members were dispatched in rescue boats whenever a storm would push a ship past the lighthouse onto the rocks. But across the years, as the ships steered by more successfully, their meetings became social gatherings and self-help classes. Instead of being a lighthouse to rescue those who were lost, their goal became fellowship and fulfillment of the membership. One night when a fierce storm drove a ship onto the rocks, they discovered that they no longer had the capacity to effectively rescue. Their boats in disrepair, their members untrained and out of shape, they stood and watched helplessly as the ship wrecked and its crew drowned.[2]

As we become more concerned with meeting the needs of members, we become deceived about what God formed us to do and be. Our communities and the people around us are experiencing one shipwreck after another, and we are not equipped to do much rescuing. Why would a drowning victim wander into my church looking for help if that person knows nothing about what happens there? And how can our members become rescuers if they are sitting in church waiting to be fed?

The "We Do Church Right" claim supposes that all of our activities and meetings are leading our members to become effective disciples. We want to think that our softball teams, music groups, men's and ladies' groups, senior adult luncheons, children's activities, and on and on, are training the rescue society to rescue the world with the gospel of Christ. Under close scrutiny, though, we may find that the purpose of all these activities is primarily fellowship and fulfillment of the membership. No wonder that some have become proponents of starting churches with nothing more than a worship service and a few home groups to avoid the trap of institutionalism. That strategy works in some settings, but it is not my intent here.

This is not a call to abandon the church and its groups and activities that we know and love. God has ordained his church as the bride of Christ. Though local churches may close their doors, God's church will triumph just as he has promised in his Word. So we must re-dream and re-structure the church to become once again the rescue society God created us to be. Our worship ministry programs must form an intentional process to equip and lead members to become worshipers on mission—disciples who are

2. This is a picture of the institutional church, and this analogy was developed by Christian dramatist Jeff Smith of Salt and Light Ministries: www.saltandlightmin.org.

actively engaged everyday leading others to become disciples. I believe this process begins with worship focused on glorifying God that engages each of us personally in discipleship and mission.

> For those who exalt themselves will be humbled, and those who humble themselves will be exalted. "Woe to you, teachers of the law and Pharisees, you hypocrites! You shut the door of the kingdom of heaven in people's faces. You yourselves do not enter, nor will you let those enter who are trying to. Matthew 23:12–13, NIV

Several dictionaries define institutionalism as "the strong attachment to established institutions." When our emotional-psychological attachment to the church establishment replaces our love for God and allegiance to the gospel, God calls it idolatry. This is a serious charge!

How can you analyze your church to determine if it is trapped in institutionalism? What clues will help you understand whether you are missional or misguided? Here are my ABCDE's of Institutionalism:

- A = Anger and Anxiety. An undercurrent of anger pervades the institution. The members are angry at the staff for not giving them the personal attention they feel they deserve. The staff is angry at the members for putting so much pressure on them to meet pastoral and program needs. Members are angry because of their inability to persuade others to agree with them on their wishes and wants. Anxiety constantly creeps into conversations about the church.
- B = Buildings and Budgets. Building maintenance and expansion consume much of the budget monies and attention of the church. Specific rooms become the property of specific classes or programs and, when called upon to share space, members become very territorial. The annual budget reflects emphasis on ministry to church members and maintenance of church property over mission to the community.
- C = Committees and Calendar. An elaborate committee system exists to maintain the organization. Consequently, the calendar is filled with meetings that leave little time for mission action and disciple-making.
- D = Disciples disappear. With an emphasis on churchmanship rather than discipleship, spiritual maturity declines steadily. Worship wars and turf wars become business-as-usual. Bible studies abound, but a clear plan to teach and train disciples and fit them into a missional strategy is nowhere to be found.

- E = Emotions and Entitlement. Members keep score on whether their wishes are being met and wear their emotions on their sleeve. Church becomes "all about me," and if individuals don't get their way you can expect an emotional outburst or pouting. Their proposed strategy is to return to the glory days of worship and programs from a former era when they were "being fed."

This predictable pattern of creeping institutionalism is as sure as the spread of the dreaded kudzu vine in the southern United States. God trims it back to unleash his salvation process, but we let it grow out of control and overwhelm the landscape all over again. John Finney, in his book, *Recovering the Past,* wrote, "Time and time again down the centuries, communities have been established with an evangelistic aim, but within a couple of generations they have become institutionalized and introverted."[3]

The "father of modern management," Peter Drucker, once said, "Any existing organization, whether a business, a church, a labor union, or a hospital, goes down fast if it does not continue to innovate . . . Not to innovate is the single largest reason for the decline of existing organizations." [4]

The church has always struggled with this process of changing to keep up. Jesus' own earthly nemesis were the Pharisees, bastion of religious institutionalism and self-preservation. The Pharisees were looking for an institutional savior to empower their institution. So they did everything in their power to protect Judaism from Jesus' influence. In the early centuries, church fathers chronicled the young Christian church in its struggle to balance mission to the outside world and ministry inside the church. In the Middle Ages, members of smaller parishes would go on pilgrimage to the cathedral, returning home to dream of how their parishes could be more like the cathedral with all its programs and events. The Reformation churches fought the same battle. One after another, courageous pastors reformed their churches from institutionalism to relevance, only to fight creeping institutionalism in their own churches again 30 to 40 years later.

In America in the 1800s and 1900s, institutionalism in the church took an interesting new turn. From the 1880s to the 1990s, evangelistic crusades featuring preachers such as D. L. Moody, Charles Finney, Billy Sunday, and Billy Graham swept across the land, producing amazing numbers of converts. These evangelistic crusades were used mightily by God to win hearts to him.

3. Finney, *Recovering the Past: Celtic and Roman Mission,* 63.

4. Drucker, *The Essential Drucker: The Best of Sixty Years of Peter Drucker's Essential Writings on Management,* 8.

But the crusades' success led many churches to adopt the crusades' pattern and theology for their worship services. Weekly worship became segmented into three parts: a song service to prepare hearts, an evangelistic gospel sermon, and the invitation to make a personal decision for Christ. The term "worship" was used commonly only to designate the music portion of the service. Decisions, rather than disciples, became the goal. Of course, the centerpiece of this worship theology is the evangelistic sermon. Consequently, the motivation for evangelical churches became getting the world to come to church so non-believers could hear the gospel preached and be won to Christ.

In the 1980s, another version of the attractional model came to the forefront of evangelical churches. It was called the seeker-sensitive model and grew out of Willow Creek Church in Chicago. Like the earlier crusade approach, seeker-sensitive worship says we should do everything we can to attract those seeking spiritual fulfillment who might be open to the gospel. Seeker-sensitive worship used pop-style songs performed by a talented band along with excellently produced drama to attract those without Christ to hear a gospel presentation by the lead pastor. The production value at Willow Creek was second to none, rivaling Broadway shows and popular television shows, as the church did everything possible to attract the outside world into the church. Concurrently, the megachurch movement of the 1980s and 1990s in American evangelical churches crystallized into huge church clubs with all of the amenities of the secular community offered inside: fitness clubs, cafes and coffee shops, concerts, focus groups, art and craft classes, and so forth.

You may ask, "What is wrong with that? Shouldn't church be attractive?" Of course, church should be attractive. But, attractional thinking is built on the belief that our primary strategy to win the world should be getting people into church. First, worship was created by God for himself, so we dare not make it first about people. True worship is all about God, glorifying him in ways that ignite us to become his worshiping disciples on mission.

Second, the statistics of decline show us that we cannot win the world with nothing but an attractional approach. We are behind now and falling further behind every day by trying to get the world into church. Yes, there will always be a percentage of churches that show amazing numerical growth. While we affirm and celebrate their growth, we must acknowledge that this will not be the pattern for most churches, especially older churches. After a number of years, fast-growth churches often find themselves facing the same creeping institutionalism and decline as neighboring churches they once ran past.

According to the Association of Religion Data Archives (www.thearda.com) the population of the United States grew 9.7 percent from 2000 to 2010, from 281,421,839 to 308,745,538. For the Christian church simply to keep up with American population growth at that same rate, we must see 27,323,699 people come to Christ over the next 10 years. But here is the astounding number: it will take 2,732 fast-growth American churches converting 1,000 a year for 10 years, just to maintain our present percentage of Christians in the population. Notice that this number is only for maintaining the Christian percentage and allows for no growth. We may get excited about fast-growth churches, but the great majority of our churches remain in decline or barely holding their own. Many of us celebrated in 2008 when we heard reports that on an average day that year, 79,000 people converted to Christ. But we quickly realized that, in the same year, the world's net growth rate was 300,000 people per day.[5]

Though we can learn from fast-growth churches, trying to replicate their blueprint may only lead to continued frustration and decline long-term. Why? Because Christ's Great Commission calls us to go to the lost world. Ultimately, while we can win some, we cannot win the world by getting them into our churches. God plans to win the world by sending the church out of the church building into the world.

In 2007, Willow Creek Church, the foremost promoter of the seeker-sensitive model of attractional worship, published *Reveal: Where Are You?* with findings from a multiple-year study of its own church programs. Willow Creek pastor Bill Hybels called the findings earth-shaking, ground-breaking, and mind-blowing." Over the years, Willow's philosophy of ministry had been: the church creates programs and activities; people participate in these activities; and the outcome is spiritual maturity. But shockingly, the report reads: "Increasing levels of participation in these sets of activities does not predict whether someone is becoming more of a disciple of Christ. It does not predict whether they love God more or they love people more."[6]

Allow me to issue a clear word of warning to church leaders and worship leaders. If we think we have cornered the market because people are knocking down the doors to get into our church, we must be very careful.

5. Mayfield, *Missional Pivot Points*, 22.

6. Hawkins and Parkinson, *Reveal: Where Are You?* Page Unknown.

If those who attend are only there to listen and leave, we are doing nothing more than perpetrating the institutional church. Our members may even be bringing their friends to worship services, and that is good, but not good enough if their intent is to sit and soak. The model may be new, but it is still institutional. It may be a leaner, simpler structure with less programs and events, but it just might be the same church-ianity we are trying so hard to flee.

Again, the call of Christ is to make disciples who make disciples. So I ask: "Do you have an intentional process in place to equip and lead your members to become worshipers on mission—disciples who are actively engaged every day leading others to become disciples, then taking them on mission?"

Today there is a missional movement sweeping through churches in America. While missions is what we do, missional is what we are. Missional is a way of seeing, thinking, and acting to grow disciples who join God in his mission to redeem the world. When I talk with churches about joining this missional movement to pour their giftedness into their communities, I am often met with resistance and skepticism. Interestingly, worship style does not seem to be a factor in the level of resistance to missional principles. The style of your worship will not make you more or less sensitive to God's call to join him in his mission. Neither will the size of the church. The issue goes deeper.

> It is easier for a camel to go through the eye of a needle than for a rich man to enter the kingdom of God. Mark 10:25, NIV

We have become rich and satisfied in our church clubs. That's how we got here to this place of decline. That's how we got off on the wrong track that's headed for a landslide. In my experience there is one primary barrier to embracing God's call to be worshipers on mission to your community. The greatest barrier to realizing the need and getting outside the church is a pre-occupation with "doing church right" as opposed to joining God in his mission to redeem the world.

A friend of mine made a presentation to a pastor and staff of a large and growing church about the call to community missions. The pastor responded after his presentation that they would not participate in this mission effort, saying, "After all, anything anyone could need, they can find in our church. We have it all right here. All they have to do is come through our doors." Strangely enough, his response was not too far removed from the pastor of the small dying church who was also at that meeting. This pastor pleaded immunity from participating in the mission effort, saying, "Our church is dying, and we need to focus all our efforts right now on self-preservation." Both of these pastors, while approaching it from vastly different angles, are leading their churches deeper into institutionalism and church-ianity.

Modern consumerism, defined as preoccupation with the self-satisfaction of consuming and discarding, has taken hold of the church today. Programs that were once designed to foster the dynamic cycle of worship-discipleship-mission have become all about us. The rescue society has become a social club.

A regional church consultant was invited to help a church participating in a program designed to revitalize churches so they can start new churches in their communities. After his presentation, a lady on the steering committee spoke up, "This is all well and good," she said, "but my question for you is how quickly can you get some other young adults into our church? I am tired of being the only person in this church in my thirties. I'll give you three months, and then I am out of here." Somehow, church members have become convinced they are customers who should be served.

In contrast, Jesus commissioned his followers to "Go and make disciples." Making disciples who go make other disciples is the core reason for our existence according to Jesus. We have built wonderful church buildings, programs, and events. But we have failed to make disciples transformed by Jesus who go make more disciples being transformed by him. As we have withdrawn from influencing the world, we have left the world to define right and wrong without the salt and light of God's Word. We are failing at the very reason for our existence as Christ's church. But we don't even know we've failed because we are so busy with church-ianity. We have tissue paper in our ears, and that tissue paper is the institutional church.

Our focus on building the institutional church as our own kingdom rather than joining God to build his kingdom can take many forms, including: being all things to all people inside the church walls, maintaining traditions we hold sacred, focusing on trying not to let our church die, and on and on. A simple, straightforward presentation entitled "Missional Church: Simple" portraying the church's institutional dilemma can be found at www.youtube.com. This white board presentation was originally produced by a local church to help its members grasp the differences between attractional and missional thinking. It shows how we have tried to attract people into church by offering the very best programs, most inspirational sermons, and exciting events. When attractional events begin to decline in participation, we undergird them with larger advertising budgets and bigger promotional campaigns. Check out the video and see how it can facilitate your understanding of missional thinking.

Institutionalism also tends to foster exclusiveness. Inside the institution everyone knows the norms for behavior, the accepted phrases and terminology, and the common organizational routine. But when an outsider comes in, they can't decipher our institutional codes that lock them out of comfortable interaction. On a recent mission trip to a Dominican Republic church, I tripped over the same unmarked step several times a day for the first four days I was there. It never failed to draw chuckles from the locals, who knew exactly where the stumbling points were and stepped around them without thinking. In the Dominican Republic they have a saying, "Because we live on an island, we think our island is the whole world." In the institutional church, we think our island is the whole world, too.

> But if you do not listen, I will weep in secret. Because of your pride; my eyes will weep bitterly, overflowing with tears, because the Lord's flock will be taken captive.
> Jeremiah 13:17, NIV

What evil force is at the heart of our battle between outward intent and inward focus? We don't have far to look to find our sin nature leering from behind the curtain. It's our pride that makes us so vulnerable to this deception and so proud of the churches we have built. Sin blinds us to what we don't know. It will continue to blind us to what God wants us to know if we leave it unchallenged.

The active letter in the word sin is always the big "I" in the middle. I want everything to be my way, to be all about me, to meet my needs first and foremost. Because earth is the battleground between God and evil, this battle will be ever-present until Jesus comes again. But God is calling us to take the tissue paper from our ears to hear and obey his call. We must confess the "I want it my way" of sin and embrace God's cleansing and freeing power.

Because each of us has our pet programs that meet our own needs and interests, we can't bring ourselves to see them change. We sit in our churches with our church friends and wonder why the world doesn't come to us. But as long as we're happy, we don't think about it too much. I will fight tooth and nail to save my pet program or event or meeting from change. This is institutional church at its worst. This is not kingdom of God thinking. But hey, we do church right! The rescue society has become a social club. The Lord's greatest missionary force is being held hostage by institutionalism and church-ianity inside the church walls. It's enough to make God weep bitterly in secret.

Return to the Cross

We sang the glorious old gospel song at the top of our lungs. It was a heartfelt response to the powerful sermon from the visiting evangelist during fall revival service.

Years I spent in vanity and pride,
Caring not my Lord was crucified,
Knowing not it was for me He died on Calvary.
Mercy there was great, and grace was free;
Pardon there was multiplied to me;
There my burdened soul found liberty At Calvary.[7]

We had worked hard to pack our pews with those who were lost in sin throughout our community. My mother and I had even gone door-to-door to invite our neighbors. But, as usual, the church was filled exclusively with loyal church members for this Tuesday night gathering of revival week. The preacher had really warmed up tonight and preached a convicting service about Jesus' sacrifice on the cross for the whole world. Too bad that none of the lost souls from our town were there to hear it. What could we do but continue to sing at the top of our voices? The frustrations we often felt about our church seemed to disappear in this moment of worship.

By God's Word at last my sin I learned;
Then I trembled at the law I'd spurned,
Till my guilty soul imploring turned To Calvary.

What was she doing? I suddenly became aware that my mother was pushing past me to get into the aisle. "Mom, are you okay?" I asked as I noticed the tears running down her cheeks. She moved quickly to the front of the church and bowed her head onto the evangelist's shoulder. What could possibly be wrong?

Now I've giv'n to Jesus ev'rything,
Now I gladly own Him as my King,
Now my raptured soul can only sing Of Calvary.

7. Newell, "At Calvary," Public Domain.

The song ended as my heart pounded in my chest. The evangelist stepped forward, his arm around my mother as she faced the congregation. "This dear sister has come forward tonight to say that she has been in this church all her life. But tonight her heart heard the gospel in a fresh, new way. She says she is tired of playing church. She realized tonight that the power of salvation is in her hands. She can share it or hoard it. She commits tonight to share the power of salvation in every way she can with the neighbors on her street. She knows she will have to do this by building relationships with them and serving them. It's going to be difficult. So she asks you to pray for her to stay in the power of the cross as she makes this effort. Let's pray right now for this dear sister."

Oh, the love that drew salvation's plan!
Oh, the grace that bro't it down to man!
Oh, the mighty gulf that God did span At Calvary.
Mercy there was great, and grace was free;
Pardon there was multiplied to me;
There my burdened soul found liberty At Calvary.

Questions for Thought and Discussion

Now that you have read this chapter, what are some things you know now that you did not realize before about your church and other churches in your community?

Analyze your church in view of the ABCDE's of institutionalism. Which of these elements of institutionalism are present in your church?

How do your church and other churches in your area reflect the evangelistic crusade and seeker-sensitive philosophies in worship? And worse, how is your church reflecting secular consumerism?

Look deep in your own heart and confess to God the points at which you have stuffed tissue in your own ears to ignore God's call to be his worshiping disciple on mission.

What would it take for you to do what the lady did in Return to the Cross and give up playing church for going on mission?

4

God Created Worship for Himself

> You shall have no other gods before me. You shall not make for yourself an idol in the form of anything in heaven above or on the earth beneath or in the waters below. You shall not bow down to them or worship them; for I, the Lord your God, am a jealous God. Exodus 20:3-5, NIV

God created worship for himself! We don't need to look any further than the first of the Ten Commandments to realize this truth. Here is almighty God telling us in no uncertain terms that he expects worship to be his and only his. You've heard it said, and may have said it yourself, "I didn't get anything out of that worship service today." But worship is not primarily for us to "get something." Instead, true worship happens when we present ourselves to God. It is all about what we bring to him.

Experiencing true worship does not result from the church building, the band, the choir, the organ, the musical style, the performers or the ministers, or any other packaging or personalities. True worship is not dependent on whether our worship is expressed in a liturgical service, an evangelical service or any other particular form or format. Worship is all about God and for God. This truth must saturate our minds and hearts to flush out any self-centeredness God finds in our worship. In *The Purpose Driven Life*, Rick Warren wrote, "True worship—bringing God pleasure—happens when you give yourself completely to God. Offering yourself to God is what worship is all about."[1]

1. Warren, *The Purpose Driven Life*, 78.

What is the core of Christian worship that is non-negotiable? What is the essence of true worship that transcends all our styles, cultures, and traditions? Is there a common worship theology that holds true regardless of denomination or local church affiliation? If we expect to embrace true worship that will power our Church Train back to our original destination, we must answer these questions. We must discover God's definition of worship that will effectively empower us as worshiping disciples on mission.

> For great is the Lord and most worthy of praise;
> he is to be feared above all gods. 1 Chronicles 16:25, NIV

Here is the main thing we need to understand if we are going to truly worship God. God does not need us. We need God. God is complete, in and of himself. His glory is not dependent on us glorifying him. He was almighty and all-glorious before creation. He was Alpha and Omega before he created us to have relationship with him. And our worship can't add one ounce to his completeness. My greatest performance does not bring value to my supremely worthy God.

The psalmist looked to the heavens and marveled at the miracle of life on this blue planet in the midst of a barren universe.

> When I consider your heavens, the work of your fingers, the moon and the stars, which you have set in place, what is man that you are mindful of him, the son of man that you care for him?" Psalm 8: 3–4, NIV.

God, the master artist, chose one single planet. Earth became the canvas for his greatest work of artistic creation—the human race. But his creative power did not stop there. God craved relationship with the people he created. When we became separated from him by our rebellious nature, he sent his son Jesus to die for our sin. Through Jesus we are eternally restored to relationship with our master creator. What a wonder!

Thomas Carlyle said, "Wonder is the basis of worship."[2] When we begin to grasp just how big God is, and how big his act of love for us, we will begin to grasp the wonder of worship. He cannot be measured, nor can he be contained. Donald Miller, in *Blue Like Jazz* wrote, "I don't think there is any better worship than wonder."[3] When we conclude that God needs us, we lose our wonder for God and replace it with familiarity. Our sinful pride

2. http://www.brainyquote.com/quotes/quotes /t/thomascarl380708.html.
3. Miller, *Blue Like Jazz*, 206.

causes us to act like we are the parent and God is a helpless child. What would he ever do without us?

There was a time in my life when I imagined God looking down on my constant effort on his behalf and proclaiming, "I sure am glad Mark Powers is on my team because he is my MVP! I don't know what I would ever do without him." What a pitiful joke I was. How misguided and ignorant of God could I have been to think such a thing? God had to break me of my ego and replace my self-worship with constant wonder for him and his awesome power.

On the other hand, God is not some self-centered, egotistical deity demanding that we constantly tell him how great he is. God does not call us to worship because he craves our adoration. He is the one true God as defined in Scripture and revealed in the person and work of Jesus Christ. It's you and I who have the need to adore him. Our worship is the expression of our relationship with him. C.S. Lewis said, "It is in the process of being worshiped that God communicates His presence to men."[4] A living, growing relationship is what he wants most of all from us. Only in the context of relationship with God can we grasp the meaning of worship.

The essence of the gospel is that our father God, who does not need us, truly does want us. He desires us not because there is any good in us, but because he is supremely good. While we were slaves of sin, God stepped up and paid the price to buy us for himself. God sent his son, Jesus, to live perfectly, die for my sin, and conquer death in his resurrection. He constantly pursues the relationship of father and child with us. This is the main teaching of Christianity that sets it apart from every other world religion: instead of humankind trying desperately to reach God, God is reaching out to us in love through Christ! How can we not respond with worship?

> Love the Lord your God with all your heart
> and with all your soul and with all your mind.
> Matthew 22:37, NIV

Our English word "worship" is derived from the Anglo-Saxon term meaning "worth-ship." Worship is the actions and attitudes that show how much we value someone or something. The simplest definition of worship is to ascribe ultimate worth. Bruce H. Leafblad reminds us, "In true worship, love is the supreme affection, and God is the exclusive object of our

4. Lewis, http://www.williamthelesser.org/quotesonworship.html.

greatest love. At its center, this divine-human encounter we call worship is a love affair of the highest and holiest order."[5]

How do you show your spouse or loved ones that you value them highly, that they are worth everything to you? Do you listen intently when they talk, engage them in conversation, lavish them with gifts, serve them, love them unconditionally, and build your relationship daily? Those are the same elements of worship which we shower upon our Lord. A.W. Tozer said: "The whole personality has to worship God. Faith, love, obedience, loyalty, high conduct and life all must be taken as burnt offerings and offered to God."[6]

In *My Utmost for His Highest*, Oswald Chambers stated: "Worship is giving God the best that He has given you. Be careful what you do with the best you have. Whenever you get a blessing from God, give it back to Him as a love gift. Take time to meditate before God and offer the blessing back to Him in a deliberate act of worship. If you hoard a thing of blessing for yourself, it will turn into spiritual dry rot, as the manna did when it was hoarded [Exodus 16]. God will never let you hold a spiritual thing for yourself, it has to be given back to Him that he may make it a blessing to others."[7]

Because worship means "worth-ship," worship is a continual lifestyle of showing God's ultimate worth 24/7, all day every day. Worship begins every morning when we present the day before us to God for his use. In my first waking moments, before I even get out of bed, I say to God, "Father, this day is yours. Take it and use it however you choose. Transform me in your image. Walk with me through every moment today and use me for your mission and your glory." This prescription for daybreak worship will ignite you to discipleship and mission as you walk in his presence throughout your day. And it will overflow into your corporate worship in church each week, too.

If we do not redefine worship as a minute-by-minute hunger for God's presence, we may think worship is all about us. How often have you heard someone say they left a church because they "just weren't being fed"? A true worshiper feeds on the presence of God 24/7 in trust and obedience. Then when we gather for corporate worship with the body of Christ, our worship

5. Leafblad, *Worship 101: Recovering the Priority of God,* http://www.ozcorners.net/worship/19-worshiparticles/30-worship-101-recovering-the-priority-of-god.

6. Snyder, *Tozer on Worship and Entertainment*, 4.

7. Chambers, *My Utmost for His Highest,* January 6: "Worship."

together is powered by our personal lifestyles of daily worship. How can I do any less if I truly accept the sacrifice of Christ on the cross for me?

So the derivation of the word "worship" helps us start to understand it. But there is more to true worship than our English word signifies. The biblical words for worship are far more descriptive and hold more meaning. Let's look at them.

> Come, let us bow down in worship, let us kneel before the Lord our Maker. Psalm 95:6, NIV

The Old Testament word for worship is the Hebrew word *shachach* (pronounced "shaw-kawh"). This word means to bow down, to fall prostrate in subjection before the one you worship.[8] When I *shachach*, I expose my neck in unguarded vulnerability. In Old Testament times the weapon of choice was the sword. If I was walking down the road and encountered a soldier in the conquering army that ruled my land, I might bow down before him. This act of submission puts my life in the hands of the approaching soldier. As I expose the nape of my neck, he can use his sword to cut off my head or stab me in the back. But on the other hand, he can turn the sword blade sideways and lay it on my shoulder to bless me, saying, "Your subjection to me has earned my favor. Rise and walk along with me. I will protect you and guide you."

In the New Testament, the word used for worship is the Greek word *proskuneo*, which means to "prostrate one's self in subjection." When we understand worship as falling before God in complete subjection, we draw closer to the heart of worship. Subjection presupposes the attitude of sacrifice, of giving up my right to myself.

In the Old Testament, sacrifice and worship were inseparable terms. King David himself once approached the altar with no sacrifice because he was at war. A bystander offered to give David his own sacrificial offering since the king did not have one himself. But David replied, "No, I insist on paying you for it. I will not sacrifice to the Lord my God burnt offerings that cost me nothing" (2 Samuel 24:24, NIV). This attitude of personal sacrifice is too often missing in our worship. Can our acts even be called worship if they cost us little or nothing? The foundation of worship is always sacrifice—God sacrificing his Son for us, us sacrificing our lives for God, and the church sacrificing personal agendas for the good of the kingdom of God.

8. Strong, *The New Strong's Exhaustive Concordance of the Bible.*

A.W. Tozer wrote, "It is certainly true that hardly anything is missing from our churches these days—except the most important thing. We are missing the genuine and sacred offering of ourselves and our worship to the God and Father of our Lord Jesus Christ."[9]

Harold Best, dean of Wheaton College Conservatory of Music, wrote: "Worship this, worship that, conferences here, symposia there; source books, methodologies, cue sheets and, sadly enough, worship styles as litmus tests for spirituality. It just may be that, instead of worshiping, we have come to the dangerous condition of worshiping about worship or even worshiping worship."[10]

Shachach and *proskuneo* paint a poignant picture of surrender and subjection to God. The primary goal of worship is not passion but surrender. In their article "We Were Made to Worship Him," Regi and Kimberlee Stone wrote: "God is simply looking for the kind of obedience that says, 'Take my finances, my abilities, my children, my home, my prayers. Use them to bless others.'" [11]

> So whether you eat or drink or whatever you do, do it all for the glory of God. 1 Corinthians 10:31, NIV

Worship is not bound by time or place. The failure to realize this concept leads to blank stares whenever I say, "Worship ignites us to discipleship and mission!" Why this reaction? Because it is so hard to think that the anemic hour of worship going on in many of our churches could ever ignite anything. We must enlarge our concept of worship!

Robert Webber, in *Worship Is a Verb,* wrote: "Worship challenges secularism because it establishes a relationship with God and sets the world in order. In worship, the good news is happening again. It reaffirms the reality of God, the significance of life, and the worth of the human person. It creates, sustains, and enhances a relationship with God, and it heals broken human relationships. Worship refreshes the soul, rekindles the spirit, and renews life."[12]

The bottom line, the main thing, the essential ingredient of true worship is this: that I hunger and thirst every moment of life for God's presence. Are you thirsting every day all day to experience God at every

9. Snyder, *Tozer on Worship and Entertainment,* 15.

10. Best, "When Is Worship Worship?" www.leaderu.com, (accessed October 8, 2008).

11. Stone and Stone, "We Were Made to Worship Him," *Perspectives on Worship: Vol 1,* 203.

12. Webber, *Worship Is a Verb,* 27.

turn? Are you hungry to find God's work revealed in daily situations and conversations? Do you possess a craving to see his glory in the smallest circumstances? This hunger for God's presence is the root of the worshiping relationship with him.

> (After the resurrection), the eleven disciples traveled to Galilee, to the mountain where Jesus had directed them. When they saw Him, they worshiped, but some doubted. Then Jesus came near and said to them, "All authority has been given to Me in heaven and on earth. Go, therefore, and make disciples of all nations, baptizing them in the name of the Father and of the Son and of the Holy Spirit, teaching them to observe everything I have commanded you. And remember, I am with you always, to the end of the age."
> Matthew 28:16–20, HCSB

Worship is first a constant lifestyle of living in the love relationship with God through Christ. Then when we gather as the body of Christ in the church, our personal worship will overflow into our corporate worship service. But a worship service is not a service to us, it is our service to God. Paul proclaimed this in Romans 12:1, translated into classic King James language, "I beseech you therefore, brethren, by the mercies of God, that ye present your bodies a living sacrifice, holy, acceptable unto God, which is your reasonable service." In the corporate worship service, the children of God gather to connect with and adore their loving heavenly Father. In a worship seminar that I attended, Robert Webber shared how worship in the family of God is like a family reunion: we greet each other on the front porch and re-establish family connection, we adore our father and celebrate our family heritage, we share stories of great moments in the life of our family, we talk of our future, we may even share a meal before we affirm our plans to stay connected with each other and our father, then we depart to represent our family name in the world.

After his resurrection, Jesus gathered his new family of believers. Before Jesus commissioned them to go make disciples and win the world for him, they fell down and worshiped him. A heart of worship will always be the ignition key for missional discipleship in the family of God. Jesus' disciples had followed him for three amazing years of ministry and then experienced the agony of his crucifixion and the joy of his resurrection. It must have been an emotional roller-coaster ride for them. There were so many things they didn't know. Now they had been summoned by Jesus to this mountain to meet with him face to face. Just as with everyone else who encountered the risen Christ, they fell down and worshiped him.

This is the first example in the New Testament of the disciples demonstrating an act of worship toward Jesus. Yes, others had worshiped Jesus during his ministry. The blind, the lame, even the lepers, had demonstrated their adoration of Jesus after he healed them. But until this moment, the New Testament has no account of his own disciples bowing in worship. Peter had made the confession of Jesus' lordship verbally, but even this confession did not lead to an act of worship on their part. Isn't it strange that the very ones who were closest to Jesus had trouble believing on a level that led to acts of personal worship? Even as they fell down and worshiped on that mountain, some of them doubted.

Disciples and worship leaders can be like that. We are so busy as a steward of the church club car that we sometimes forget to worship him ourselves. We desperately need to hear a fresh call to authentic corporate worship that ignites discipleship and mission.

> These people honor me with their lips, but their heart is far from me. They worship me in vain; their teachings are but rules taught by men. Matthew 15:8–10, NIV

The worship renewal movement began several decades ago to rediscover the place of authentic corporate worship in our evangelical church life. For centuries, evangelicals had been so focused on evangelism that we had ignored communing and connecting with the Father in our worship services. Worship in our churches had become primarily evangelistic services focused on attracting non-believers into church to hear the gospel. In that setting, only the music portion of the service was referred to as worship, like an appetizer for the main course—the sermon.

Worship in the church should not be defined by our music. The power of church is not the power of music. The power to change the world does not come from a particular musical style. In fact, in a typical worship service, only 15 to 30 minutes are given to music. If you do the math, that means that around two tenths of one percent of the 10,080 minutes of a churchgoers' whole week is spent engaged in worship music. How strange that, in many churches, 100 percent of our identity is determined by two-tenths of a percent of our weekly activity. "The major challenge," according to George Barna, "is not about how to use music to facilitate worship as much as it is to help people understand worship and have an intense passion to connect with God."[13] Bryan Spinks has said: "To put it bluntly, worship is about worshiping God and the Lamb, and not about entertaining the sheep!"[14]

The focus of biblical worship has always been God initiating relationship with a chosen people at the cost of his Son on the cross. This revelation demands a corporate response of self-denial and sacrifice. But attractional worship mistakenly turns the spotlight of worship on individuals and meeting their "felt needs" in a worship service. The danger here is that worship with the family of God becomes our individual narcissistic relationship with God, like the child at the family reunion who seizes all the attention as if they were the only one present. In that self-focused context, corporate worship becomes simply a party or show the church offers me. Then, few demands, if any, are placed on seekers since it becomes the church's responsibility to sell them on the benefits of following God. Shallow worship produces shallow Christians who are no more than consumers of worship as entertainment. And worse, worship narcissism can fuel ruthless church leaders who tear apart the church with their own agenda on committees or governing boards in the institutional church. Paul warned Timothy of people "having a form of godliness but denying its power" (2 Timothy 3:1–5, NIV). Acceptance of Christ is always a personal decision of surrender at the heart level. And discipleship focuses on continued surrender in daily life. Sending church members on mission may be the best antidote to our self-centeredness. In the meantime, God's kingdom is seriously hindered by self-centered worshipers who are allowed to think worship is "all about me."

Bob Kauflin, in his book, *Worship Matters: Leading Others to Encounter the Greatness of God,* stated the biblical concept of worship beautifully: "Worship is God's gift of grace to us before it is our offering to God. Apart from this perspective, leading worship can become self-motivated and self-exalting. We subtly take pride in our worship, our singing, our playing, our planning, our performance, our leadership. Unfortunately we separate ourselves from the God who drew us to worship him in the first place. Gathering to praise God cannot be a means to some "greater" end, such as church growth, evangelism, or personal ministry. God is not a genie we summon by rubbing the bottle called 'worship.' He doesn't exist to help us get where we really want to go. He is where we want to go. God's glory is

13. "Focus on 'Worship Wars' Hides the Real Issues Regarding Connection to God," www.barna.org, (accessed November 19, 2002).

14. Spinks, "Worshipping the Lamb or Entertaining the Sheep," www.modernreformation.org, (accessed July 31, 2012).

the end of our worship, and not simply a means to something else. In the midst of a culture that glorifies our pitiful accomplishments in countless ways, we gather each week to proclaim God's wondrous deeds and to glory in His supreme value."[15]

The worship renewal movement was long overdue. But, as often the case in renewal, we focus solely on the area which is crying out for attention and are blinded to other issues. "Let's fix this problem," we say, and we pour all our attention and resources into solving that issue. By focusing exclusively on worship, we have given it disproportionate attention. It seems that we think we will fix the church if we can just fix our worship. If we are not careful, the focal issue of worship becomes our newest idol. The goal of this book is certainly to renew our worship. But it goes beyond that to show you how worship is just the start of the church's calling. My passion is that you will see that worship—both personal worship and corporate worship—is the ignition key to discipleship and that you will learn how the power of true worship propels us out to share Christ with the world around us.

When all is said and done, we have nothing to offer our world but God himself and his Son, our Savior. Jesus, our only source of power to impact the world, mandates that we "Go" and share his power with the world. Yet we keep on missing it. At a recent conference, Charles Billingsley, worship leader at Thomas Road Baptist Church in Lynchburg Va., said, "God doesn't need our production to show his presence. True worship is not just what we do; true worship is what we are."[16] We think if we can just offer the right mix of music presented by outstanding performers enhanced with modern technology that true worship will result. We are very flashy, but often very empty. If our worship is not focused totally on God, it will be essentially powerless in eternal impact. After all, he created it for himself!

Return to the Cross

And can it be that I should gain
An interest in the Savior's blood?
Died He for me, who caused His pain?
For me, who Him to death pursued?
Amazing love! How can it be
That thou, my God, should die for me?[17]

15. Kauflin, *Worship Matters: Leading Others to Encounter the Greatness of God*, 176–77.
16. Author's personal conversation with Charles Billingsley.
17. Wesley, "And Can It Be," Public Domain.

Life hurts. Dad develops a malicious lung condition which steadily drains life. Mother-in-law is silently overcome by Alzheimer's, a slow goodbye to awareness. Betrayal invades a marriage, and loved ones divorce. Where are you God? Are you real? Or are you just an idea cooked up by desperate humans afraid of insignificance in a lonely universe? Question marks abound in life.

He left his Father's throne above,
So free, so infinite His grace;
Emptied Himself of all but love,
And bled for Adam's helpless race;
'Tis mercy all, immense and free;
O praise my God, it reaches me.

Reach me, Lord. Can you reach me? I am desperate to feel the wonder of your presence. Doubt threatens, but faith yearns to rise and lift me to you. Be merciful and free me from captivity to self.

Long my imprisoned spirit lay
Fast bound in sin and nature's night;
Thine eye diffused a quick'ning ray,
I woke, the dungeon flamed with light;
My chains fell off, my heart was free;
I rose, went forth, and followed thee.

Your light invades; darkness runs to the shadows. Strength overtakes weakness; healing overcomes pain. Lord, I worship you!

No condemnation now I dread;
Jesus and all in Him is mine!
Alive in Him, my living Head,
And clothed in righteousness divine,
Bold I approach the eternal throne,
And claim the crown, thro' Christ, my own.
Amazing love!
How can it be that thou, my God, should die for me?

Questions for Thought and Discussion

If you asked the average church member in today's evangelical church, "Who created worship?" what would their answer most likely be? If you asked them, "Who was worship created for?" how would they probably answer?

How should the understanding that God created worship for himself impact our weekly worship experience? How should this understanding impact our daily life?

Is there a time in your life when God has broken you of your tendency to think that God needs you and your worship? What would it take for you to be broken like that and reclaim the wonder of worship?

How should the biblical concepts of *shacach* and *proskuneo* impact our worship services?

Imagine yourself on the mountain of ascension face to face with our resurrected Lord. What do you see, hear, and feel among the crowd of followers gathered there? When Jesus appears before you, what is your personal response? Describe your feelings and thoughts as you hear Jesus' command to "Go."

5

When Methodology Becomes Idolatry

> Away with the noise of your songs! I will not listen to the music of your harps. But let justice roll on like a river, righteousness like a never-failing stream! Amos 5:23-24, NIV

I HAVE FRIENDS WHO travel the country as consultants for church growth with churches of every denomination, size, and style. I ask them: "What do you see across America in worship?"

Many have replied: "Worship idolatry is rampant in the church today. Most worship leaders in our churches are little more than performers putting on a good show."

Does God need us to put on a really great show to sell him to the masses? Is he just waiting in the wings for some help from my worship team? Is God nervously hoping that his people will somehow "get something" out of our worship service? Has God postponed winning the world until all our church members are happy with the music and preaching? We have taken the King of the universe, the creator of all things, and cast him as a pleading old man who begs us to come to him.

Over the last two chapters we have mapped the institutional-attractional track that the Church Train has followed to get on the wrong track. Next we defined the essence of authentic worship that transcends style and denominationalism. Now it is time to take a hard look at our worship to identify sources of idolatry.

Recently, I had a heart scan. The heart scan shows everything in my heart without threatening my health. My family history is genetically marked with heart disease. Our human family is marked with heart disease called sin. We need a daily heart scan to measure our worship lifestyle by God's standard. May this chapter be our heart scan.

> Who makes a god or casts a metal image for no profit? Look, all its worshipers will be put to shame, and the craftsmen are humans. Isaiah 44:10–11, HCSB

Bob Kauflin said on his Worship Matters blog: "When someone mentions idolatry, we can picture some tribesman in New Guinea bowing down to statues of wood or metal, and think, 'Thank God I don't struggle with THAT.' Idols, however, are far more pervasive, insidious, and deceptive. Idolatry is attributing ultimate value, authority, or supremacy to any object other than God. Whenever I think I can't worship God unless "X" is present, I'm making a profound statement. If "X" is anything other than Jesus Christ and the Holy Spirit, I've moved into idolatrous territory. Idolatry is always evil, but the idols we pursue aren't necessarily evil things. They are evil for us because we value them over God."[1]

Let's be honest. Whether as worshiper in the audience or worship leader on the platform, the temptation of idolatry grips us all. We project our personalities above God's glory. We present performances in place of broken and contrite hearts. We replace proclamation of God's Word with positive-thinking techniques. It's easy to depend on personal charm and skill to draw a crowd. But God always calls us to be reflections of his glory, not enamored with our own glory. Paul said in 1 Corinthians 2:1–5: "When I came to you, brothers, I did not come with eloquence or superior wisdom . . . For I resolved to know nothing while I was with you except Jesus Christ and him crucified . . . My message and my preaching were not with wise and persuasive words, but with a demonstration of the Spirit's power, so that your faith might not rest on men's wisdom, but on God's power." (NIV) God will not overlook anything we put in his place of glory, especially if that thing is me.

According to the Great Commission, engaging in worship services is not the essential work of the church. When we make weekly worship an end in itself, we are easily tempted to worship the very acts of worship. We are tempted to worship our favorite style of worship. We are tempted to worship our most meaningful experience of worship. And when we worship the acts of worship, we are missing the only worthy object of worship—God

1. Kauflin, "Idolatry on Sunday Mornings, Pt. 1." No pages.

incarnate in Christ manifested in the Holy Spirit. If we worship the way we "do" worship, our methodology has become idolatry.

When Jesus gathered his followers on the mountain he did not say, "Go ye, therefore, and worship." Worship is not an end in itself! Worship is a means to an end. What is that end, that ultimate goal? Jesus' commission to the church is to make disciples and win the world, pure and simple. Jesus' followers fell down and worshiped him, but then they arose and moved out into the world to make disciples. Our commission from Christ is to win the world by making disciples for him. Worship idolatry has become a huge distraction from the process of making disciples who make disciples.

> Then Jesus said to His disciples, "If anyone wants to come with Me, he must deny himself, take up his cross, and follow Me." Matthew 16:24, HCSB

In a world separated from God, daily life becomes a web of cravings for personal happiness. Western culture has elevated our selfish cravings to be socially acceptable and even admired. Morality has become "what makes me happy right now" rather than a behavioral standard set by God. This culture of self-satisfaction is a trap to Christian worshipers. And the Evil One has set that trap just for you and me. Oh, how many times I have fallen into it myself. We want to be the standard by which things around us are measured. We want attention and praise and glory. Even in subtle ways we crave to have the focus on ourselves. As we humble ourselves to pray we wonder who noticed us kneeling.

In many of our churches, the absence of an intentional discipleship process leaves church members with no other frame of reference than themselves. They think they are doing the right thing because their only reference is their personal preference. But preference is only an extension of self. To enthrone my preference as the only way it should be done is to put myself on the throne of worship.

A young worship leader who I have mentored for many years was called to appear before his church's personnel committee. On the table around which they were gathered lay his job description. One of his many responsibilities read: "Provide worship that will edify the church members and connect young families in our community with God."

In that sentence only the first seven words had been highlighted by the chairwoman of the committee. "We have called you here to tell you that you are not meeting the worship needs of the people on this committee," she stated.

The young worship leader reminded them that he was presenting traditional hymns as well as songs in modern styles. Then he had the audacity to ask why the second half of the phrase was not highlighted. The chairwoman spoke up, "We are not here to talk about those other people. We are the financial supporters and workers in this church, and your job is to give us what we want."

Of course, it's easy for worship leaders to point an accusing finger at church members. We blame our members for holding us back from true worship. But we worship leaders are not immune to idolatry. We become the self-appointed local authority on worship. We develop a worship plan and style that keeps our members happy; then we deify that order of worship. Or we may be worshiping our own personal preference for classical works or contemporary choruses or Southern gospel songs or hymns. Who are we to stand before God and tell him what he needs?

Judson Cornwall, in his book *Worship as Jesus Taught It*, wrote: "Whenever the method of worship becomes more important than the Person of worship, we have already prostituted our worship. There are entire congregations who worship praise and praise worship but who have not yet learned to worship God in Jesus Christ".[2]

> But I, when I am lifted up from the earth, will draw all men to myself. John 12:32, NIV

Look at Jesus' words from John 12:32. This statement is rich with meaning on many levels. First, Jesus was reminding his Hebrew listeners how Moses lifted up the serpent in the wilderness as a sign of healing. In this reference, Jesus built a bridge both to his Jewish heritage and to his crucifixion to come. Just as Moses lifted up the serpent, Jesus would soon be lifted up on a Roman cross as the ultimate healer of sin for all time and all eternity. But there is more in this simple statement that we dare not miss. Jesus was also giving us the simplest formula for true worship. When we lift him up above all, he will draw hearts and lives to himself. Worship style is simply packaging for the truth of the gospel.

I have used the same brand of body lotion for many years. Across those years, the identifying marks of the lotion bottle—color, shape, print style, etc.—seldom change. And why would it, since the manufacturers want me to be able to identify it easily in any store? On the other hand, the words "new and improved" seem to appear on my lotion regularly. They are always seeking to change the product to better fit the ever-changing needs of the users.

2. Cornwall, *Worship as Jesus Taught It*, 70.

The good news that Christ died on the cross for the sin of the world is just the opposite from my favorite lotion. The product of the gospel is never new and improved. When Christ gave his life for us, it was fully active for all time and all people in all places. Truth, by definition, is completely true and never gets stronger, more effective, or "more true." Christ's death and resurrection cannot be improved upon. It always will be the only way that God redeems us to himself. God's plan is perfect.

But our tendency, like the manufacturer of my lotion, is to make an icon of the packaging. Any way you cut it, our music and preaching styles, architecture, dress, seating arrangement, format, etc. are simply packaging for the product. We want to take our favorite shape, color, and style and make them the standard in every market. When we fall into that trap, worship methodology becomes idolatry. Worship of God misses the mark when we make it all about our favorite package. The formula for real worship is all about the product—the gospel—not the packaging.

Rick Warren wrote in *The Purpose Driven Church*: "Every church likes to believe its worship style is the most biblical. The truth is there isn't a biblical style of worship. Each Sunday true believers around the world give glory to Jesus Christ using a thousand equally valid expressions and styles."[3] Colossians 3:16 (NIV) shows us that God affirms variety in our worship: "Let the Word of God dwell in you richly with all wisdom, teaching and admonishing one another with psalms, hymns, and spiritual songs, giving thanks in your hearts to God." In modern terms, psalms are Scripture songs, hymns are great songs of the faith that present the gospel, and spiritual songs are songs sung to God personally.

If the gospel never changes, why should the packaging of the gospel change? The language and style of our cultural context at any given time demand different wrappers. The means of communicating the truth of the gospel must be contextualized to best convey the message. The means of salvation, however, will always be Jesus Christ, Son of God.

> When a woman who had lived a sinful life in that town learned that Jesus was eating at the Pharisee's house, she brought an alabaster jar of perfume, and as she stood behind him at his feet weeping, she began to wet his feet with her tears. Then she wiped them with her hair, kissed them and poured perfume on them. Luke 7:37–39, NIV

3. Warren, *The Purpose Driven Church*, 241.

God originated excellence as he made this marvelous universe. Then God showed omnipotent creativity as he lovingly formed us and placed us in this awesome world. What an excellent creation of his we are!

God wants us to reflect his creative excellence as *imagio dei*, the image of God. In his image all humans are made to create. A Christian artist has a distinctive calling and gifting from God to create. Excellence is how we both honor the gift God has given us and fulfill his call to glorify him with it. Yes, we should hone our craft to the highest level as we offer it to God. When we use our gifts to create with excellence, we reflect God's excellence. God uses our creative excellence to glorify himself in three ways:

1. Providing us the abundant life Jesus promised when we live in Him,
2. Serving and equipping the body of Christ, his church, and
3. Calling the world to redemption in Christ through excellent creative arts.

Excellence is our worthy gift to God.

Can artistic excellence become an idol? Yes. Excellence can easily become an end-in-itself. Excellence must never be a means of placing our artistic ability on the throne of worship. When the woman poured oil on Jesus' feet, her expression of love was extravagant. Our gift of worship excellence is our extravagant gift. We pour it out on Jesus because we owe him everything, never to earn praise for our own ability.

Let's put excellence in its proper place. Are we extravagant, pouring out our artistic gifts in excellence to him? Redefine excellence as extravagant worship for our Father who loves us extravagantly.

> For the desire to do what is good is with me, but there is no ability to do it. For I do not do the good that I want to do, but I practice the evil that I do not want to do.
> Romans 7:18–19, HCSB

In spite of our desire to do good, we continue falling into idolatry in our worship. The two most prominent symptoms of worship idolatry that I encounter in my own life, and in the lives of worship leaders and worshipers around me, are indulging in performance pride and becoming the self-appointed keeper of standards. Let's look at these two temptations that so easily entrap us.

Performance Pride

The tools of artistic expression have immense power. Like all tools, the artistic tools of music, art, drama, and movement can be used for powerful good or for malicious evil. God gives us these tools both to accomplish his work and for our personal enrichment. Performance is simply the medium through which these tools become active and are expressed.

Our society adores the American Idol mentality. Rock-star status is cultivated throughout our society. Flashy athletes get the headlines. Celebrities reign supreme in the media and are marketed to a star-hungry population. A distinctive performance style delivered with passion can be a ticket to stardom, if you have the celebrity connections. In the world, performance is everything.

But, American "me-ology" is in direct conflict with Christian theology. In biblical worship, performance fulfills only two God-given purposes. First, performance in church is the medium through which we express worship to our sovereign Lord. Second, performance is the medium through which we communicate the gospel. That's all—no more, no less. Performance in church should not be a ticket to stardom or celebrity status. It is not meant to impress or entertain anyone. There is only one "star" in worship, and he is our eternal God.

Self-centered pride always undermines our God-given purpose in life. Pride is at the root of our sin nature. If we are honest, we acknowledge that pride plagues us even in worship. We secretly hope we are being noticed for our platform style. We wonder if anyone appreciated how eloquent and heart-felt our prayer was. We crave compliments for our musical offerings. We love recognition.

While it may not seem so, the performance mentality is giving in to salvation by works. We think our performance will gain more grace, more favor, more acclaim. But God already loves us to the fullest extent possible. Absolutely nothing we do can earn more of God's love. He loves us totally and completely. He sent his very own Son to die for us on a cross of love. Absolutely nothing we do can earn that gift, not even a great performance.

A corollary to this for a worship leader is personal pride in my performers. Using people as fuel for my Church Train is just as idolatrous as personal performance pride. We stoke the Church Train engine with them until they are burned up. Too often we allow ourselves to think of our worship team members only in terms of what they can do for us. My reputation is at stake in the quality of their abilities and performance. But when

I elevate my own reputation above the well-being of fellow worship team members, I have once again dethroned God to replace him with me.

> Therefore, I urge you, brothers, in view of God's mercy, to offer your bodies as living sacrifices, holy and pleasing to God—this is your spiritual act of worship. Do not conform any longer to the pattern of this world, but be transformed by the renewing of your mind. Then you will be able to test and approve what God's will is—his good, pleasing and perfect will. Romans 12:1–2, NIV

Keeper of Standards

The keeper of standards appoints himself Supreme Court justice of all things worship. The keeper of standards is one who has forgotten that they are a sinner too. I confess that I have been guilty of this practice. And so have you. We attempt to play God. But there is only one God, and I am not him. Neither are you.

No worship leader is exempt from the temptation to lift up false standards. We are all vulnerable. I see contemporary worship leaders who despise traditional musicians for their purist conceit; yet they do the same with modern style and song. I see traditional musicians who elevate subjective standards to the level of divine. I see Southern gospel fans who are as snobbish as those who think only hymns are appropriate in worship. What standard have you placed on the worship throne? What have you elevated to the level of idol? I know mine. Do you know yours?

God despises idolatry of any kind. A worship leader is not allowed to absorb even a ray of God's glory for his or her own pride. Somehow we have convinced ourselves that our experience and training give us the inside track. We are sure that we know more than anyone in our church—and more than most of our fellow worship leaders for that matter. We are convinced that the church owes us big-time thanks. We have convinced ourselves that we are doing God a great favor by exalting a stylistic standard. But stylistic standards are based on externals, whereas God is looking deep within.

Where can we find God's standard for authentic worship? We find his standard only in his Word. And the Word of God is surprisingly inclusive of worship style. Instead of worship externals, God's focus is the activity of the heart throughout every moment of worship. God is running a continuous heart scan on each of us.

It is so easy for us to squelch the power of authentic worship by becoming keepers of the standard. Jesus harshest words were aimed at Pharisees who held the truth at arm's length so they could hold tight to religious power. Am I a Pharisee? Jesus shines a searchlight into our hearts that reveals our deepest intentions. He tests our inner core to seek out selfish pride. There is false security for us in playing God. It sets us above others and gives us a false sense of control. After all, life is very insecure. Death lurks daily. Health can come and go in a moment. Nothing is assured. Judging others by our own standards can certainly make us feel secure. But, it is pernicious pride at its worst.

These are hard words. I know as you read this you may feel under attack. You may feel defensive and possibly angry. You may feel that this is an affront to your integrity as a Christian. If that is how you feel, I beg you to look deep inside your own heart. Let these words sink into your soul and be used by God. We must submit to the laser beam of God's judgment. We must develop a standard that goes beyond our own preferences. When all is said and done, whether we have lifted up our crucified Christ above everything else is the standard that matters most.

> . . the glorious wealth of this mystery, which is Christ in you, the hope of glory. Colossians 1:27, HCSB

We must look carefully to see if we are caught up in performance pride or have appointed ourselves as keeper of standards. Our selfish nature and our heart for God are always at war within us. If we are ever going to experience victory in that inner war, we have to aggressively call our own hand at self-centeredness. We must develop inner referees that will "throw the flag" when we are off-sides. Every worship leader on your team must be practicing the spiritual disciplines of prayer and Bible study every day. You as leader must model those disciplines and hold your team accountable to eliminate self-centeredness. In every moment and in every action we must ask ourselves: "Am I lifting anything above Jesus? Are there any idols in my life or in our worship that would block attention from him?" Then periodically we need to engage in more intense searching and self-examination in a retreat setting. A day away from the office alone with God can revolutionize your relationship with our Lord. Calendar a personal retreat monthly, quarterly, or at the very least annually.

Once again, allow me to remind us that the ultimate antidote for idolatry is a craving to experience the presence of God in each moment of life. When I deeply desire to know God's presence, life tends to order itself according to his purpose in surrender and obedience. Are we more hungry and thirsty to see God's amazing presence every day than we are to get our own way?

While touring a Colonial reenactment site, I saw the silversmith melting silver over a small flame. He explained that he was heating the molten silver until he could see his reflection in it. At that point, he would know that he had melted away the impurities and could use it to make fine jewelry. We must allow God to melt away our impurities in the heat of his flame. Self-assessment, tested by the heat of God's Word, helps us maintain purity—not of musical preference—but of our passion for God. When our passion for God is pure, our worship will reflect his image and not ours.

Return to the Cross

I hear the Savior say, "Thy strength indeed is small,
Child of weakness, watch and pray,
Find in me thine all in all."
Jesus paid it all,
All to Him I owe;
Sin had left a crimson stain,
He washed it white as snow.[4]

When I stand at the foot of the cross and I look up at Jesus—his body torn and his heart broken for my sin—a thought overwhelms me. The power of the cross goes far beyond imitation. I cannot live the Christ life by copying what Jesus might do. I must die. When self is dead, then and only then is there room for Christ in my life.

For nothing good have I
Whereby Thy grace to claim;
I'll wash my garments white
In the blood of Calv'ry's Lamb.

In Christ's death he shows me how to die for him. In his resurrection I am reborn. Once, we were worlds away from each other—I in my sin and

4. Hall, "Jesus Paid It All," Public Domain.

he in his heaven. Then God came to us. The truth of his undeniable love is this: God has given Jesus for my sin, he now lives in me.

Jesus paid it all,
All to Him I owe;
Sin had left a crimson stain,
He washed it white as snow.

Lord, put to death my idolatrous ego and use me for your glory. You bought me; I am yours; take full possession. Plant yourself in the center of my heart and grow from the inside out. I surrender to you my worship preferences that have become idolatrous. Take them off the throne and take your rightful place as King. You alone are the object of my worship.

Questions for Thought and Discussion

Be truly honest with yourself. When you peel back the layers of religious thought, what is your personal image of God? Can our image of God cause us to fall into worship idolatry?

Name three ways our secular culture of self-promotion has invaded the attitudes of our church members. Name five elements of worship methodology that have become idols in your church.

Do you see performance pride evident in worshipers and worship leaders around you? Where do you see it in your own life?

Do you see self-appointed keepers of standards around you? Where do you see that tendency in your own life?

What is God's true standard of worship?

6

The Circle of Missional Living: Worship—Discipleship—Mission

Meanwhile, Saul was still breathing out murderous threats against the Lord's disciples. He went to the high priest and asked him for letters to the synagogues in Damascus, so that if he found any there who belonged to the Way, whether men or women, he might take them as prisoners to Jerusalem. As he neared Damascus on his journey, suddenly a light from heaven flashed around him. He fell to the ground and heard a voice say to him, "Saul, Saul, why do you persecute me?"

"Who are you, Lord?" Saul asked.

"I am Jesus, whom you are persecuting," he replied. "Now get up and go into the city, and you will be told what you must do." Acts 9:1-6, NIV

WHO IS THE GREATEST missionary of the first century Christian church? The apostle Paul gets the unanimous vote. Here is a man who made a name for himself by persecuting and arresting Christians. His birth name was Saul of Tarsus and he had learned Jewish theology from Gamaliel, the most noted Hebrew scholar of the day. Paul was present and supportive of the Jewish religious rulers who killed Stephen, an early Christian leader.

One day Saul headed to Damascus to arrest a group of Christians there. On the road, Jesus spoke directly to him from a blinding cloud of light, calling him to make a 180-degree life-change. Saul fell cowering before the glory of the Lord. In that encounter God gave Saul a new name: Paul; and a new identity: apostle. The apostle Paul spent the remainder of his life making Christ known to the people groups of his world. The one who had avidly persecuted Christians now endured persecution for his own faith in Christ. As the first Christian missionary, Paul carried the gospel across the known world of his day. His do-or-die aim in life became to make disciples who make disciples.

Paul modeled the circle of missional living that should define our lives. Paul's missional calling began with personal worship that fueled discipleship that led to his zeal for the mission of Christ. Let's see how this circle is reflected in two passages from Paul's New Testament writings. In both of these passages a high moment of worship was followed immediately by a direct call to discipleship. We often miss this progression, however, because the passages occur across chapter divisions in our modern Bible. The progression is lost as we stop at the chapter breaks. Paul's original writing was a continuous letter with no break in thought. Let's look at these passages as originally intended, as one flowing thought.

Worship: Romans 11:33-36, HCSB

Oh, the depth of the riches both of the wisdom and the knowledge of God! How unsearchable His judgments and untraceable His ways! For who has known the mind of the Lord? Or who has been His counselor? Or who has ever first given to Him, and has to be repaid? For from Him and through Him and to Him are all things. To Him be the glory forever. Amen.

Discipleship: Romans 12:1-6, HCSB

Therefore, brothers, by the mercies of God, I urge you to present your bodies as a living sacrifice, holy and pleasing to God; this is your spiritual worship. Do not be conformed to this age, but be transformed by the renewing of your mind, so that you may discern what is the good, pleasing, and perfect will of God. For by the grace given to me, I tell everyone among you not to think of himself more highly than he should think. Instead, think sensibly, as God has distributed a measure of faith to each one.

Paul's personal expression of worship is a beautiful lyric proclaiming God's all-encompassing power. We see here that Paul was first a true worshiper. He understood that worship is only for God and his glory. Paul demonstrated a purity of focus on God that truly defines worship. Then Paul's worship flowed into a compelling call to discipleship that ignited his heart for missions. His missional heart then empowered his personal worship, starting the circle in motion again. This cycle of worship-discipleship-mission was as natural as breathing to Paul.

Read these verses again and let them speak directly to you. Can you hear God's call to worship him? Can you hear God's call to discipleship? Can you hear God's call to become a worshiping disciple on mission?

Let's look at another passage in which Paul followed this same progression:

Worship: Ephesians 3:14-21, HCSB

I bow my knees before the Father from whom every family in heaven and on earth is named.

[I pray] that He may grant you, according to the riches of His glory, to be strengthened with power through His Spirit in the inner man, and that the Messiah may dwell in your hearts through faith.

[I pray that] you, being rooted and firmly established in love, may be able to comprehend with all the saints what is the length and width, height and depth of God's love, and to know the Messiah's love that surpasses knowledge, so you may be filled with all the fullness of God. Now to Him who is able to do above and beyond all that we ask or think—according to the power that works in you—to Him be glory in the church and in Christ Jesus to all generations, forever and ever. Amen.

Discipleship: Ephesians 4:1-3, HCSB

I, therefore, the prisoner in the Lord, urge you to walk worthy of the calling you have received, with all humility and gentleness, with patience, accepting one another in love, diligently keeping the unity of the Spirit with the peace that binds [us].

Again, we see an expression of true worship followed by a call to discipleship. In each of the above examples the word, "therefore," is a trampoline that propels us from powerful worship into the call to personal discipleship.

I propose to you that the circle of missional living for all Christians is worship-discipleship-mission. We must understand that the worship-discipleship-mission cycle is not a step-by-step, one-two-three process. These three elements flow into each other and yet are inter-connected. Each element continually gives meaning to the others. When we grasp what true worship is, it will deepen our discipleship. When we grow deeper in discipleship, we will worship more authentically. True worship and discipleship compel us to join God on mission. When we join God everyday and every moment on mission, the results flow back into worship and discipleship. Can you comprehend how these three elements should work in the Christian life?

Here is how that circle worked in Paul's life: Paul the missionary was first and foremost a worshiper of God. His worship expressed his deep, transforming love for God. This all-encompassing love led him to yield to God as student and follower. Then, as a disciple, his life overflowed into missionary action. In turn, Paul's discipleship and mission energized his worship. May we too experience the continuous circle of worship-discipleship-mission flowing to worship-discipleship-mission.

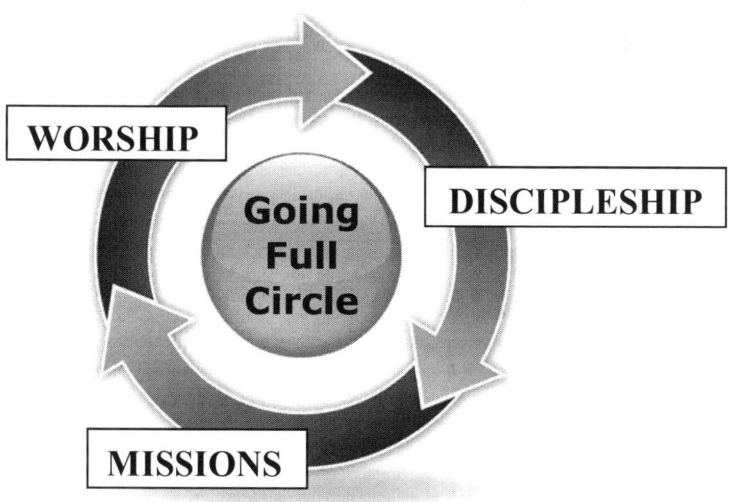

Diagram 1

Going Full Circle

The worship-discipleship-mission circle is at the center of this book because this cycle is the axis of the Christian life. In the circle of missional living we find the basic process Jesus used to train his disciples. Indeed, this circle is the foundation of the New Testament and a summary of the Great Commission. And today, as we face the decline of the evangelical church, worship-discipleship-mission is the key to restoring the intent and purpose of our churches. If we want our worship heightened and our discipleship deepened, we must be on mission all the time. Please do not miss this! I truly believe that God is telling his church that we can recapture our purpose, our energy, and our focus when we go full circle with missional living.

Have you experienced the dynamic power the circle of missional living gives our lives? If so, then here is a crucial question: Why have we allowed these three elements to become divorced from each other, isolated and compartmentalized in the institutional church? Think about it. We define worship as that hour or so every week we spend at church in a worship service. Discipleship has been reduced to the number of video studies we've attended. And missions is sending someone else to a foreign country. As my friend Curt Watke has asked, "How many video Bible studies do you need before you will speak to your next door neighbor who doesn't know Jesus?"

> In fact, though by this time you ought to be teachers, you need someone to teach you the elementary truths of God's word all over again. You need milk, not solid food!
> Hebrews 5:12, NIV

Worship leaders, what is Jesus' primary calling to us? If Jesus' highest calling to the church is to make disciples, is that not our calling too? Is that not the measuring stick for our ministries and our lives, and even our worship? The obvious answer to this question is, "Yes." My ultimate calling as a worship leader is to make disciples for my Lord Jesus Christ. Because this is the church's ultimate calling, this is also a worship leader's ultimate calling.

Yet we struggle with this concept. Our traditional training has led us to believe that worship leaders only provide worship experiences. We leave discipleship to the pastor, education minister, or Bible-teaching organization of our church. Discipleship in the institutional church is too often only a training program for churchmanship. Our strategy for equipping good church members is to fill them with information and hope they become disciples. Then we define discipleship by how many church activities they attend. We have missed the point. Real discipleship is far more.

The Greek word for disciple is *mathetes,* which literally means "learner." Discipleship is our ongoing human response of attitude and action to Christ's revelation of the eternal God of the universe. That sounds like the definition of worship too, doesn't it? The thesaurus equates a disciple to one who would be a "follower, believer, devotee, and student." Webster's dictionary defines disciple as "one who accepts and assists in spreading the doctrines of another." And that sounds like the definition of a missionary. By definition, worship, discipleship, and mission overflow into each other.

But these secular definitions still miss the essence of Christian discipleship. Simply put, to become a disciple of Jesus Christ is to be totally transformed by him. Christian discipleship is not just behavior modification. True discipleship is more than information accumulation or conforming to a standard. Christian discipleship is nothing less than being totally transformed every day by God in Christ through the power of the Spirit. "He changes the fabric of people's beings. He brings light to darkness. He brings death to life. He brings old to new. The transformation Jesus offers is radically different . . . Transformation is more than a surface-level alteration: it's actually becoming something else entirely."[1]

A Christian disciple is one whose main goal is to be continually transformed by Christ through the indwelling of the Holy Spirit every day. Are the participants on your worship team being transformed into disciples? Are the worshipers in your church true disciples? How can you tell?

In the book *The Emotionally Healthy Church*, authors Pete Scazzero and Warren Bird identify the levels of Christian spiritual maturity in terms of human emotional development from infant to adult. Here are excerpts from their descriptions of the levels of emotional maturity:

- Emotional Infant=I am perceived as self-centered. I look for others to take care of me more than I look to take care of them. I am consistently driven by a need for instant gratification. I am unaware how my behavior is affecting others.
- Emotional Child=When life is going my way and I am receiving all the things I want and need, I am content and seem emotionally well-adjusted. When I don't get my way, I often complain, throw a temper tantrum, withdraw, manipulate, etc. I interpret disagreements as a personal offense.

1. Geiger, *Transformational Discipleship*, 9.

- Emotional Adolescent=I know the right ways I should behave, but I can feel threatened when I am offered constructive criticism. I subconsciously keep records on the love I give out, so I can ask for something in return later. I am primarily committed to self-survival so I have trouble hearing another person's needs.
- Emotional Adult=I respect and love others without having to change them. I take responsibility for my own thoughts and actions. I am able to accurately assess my limits and discuss them with others. I am deeply convinced that I am absolutely loved by Christ, so I have nothing to prove. In tune with my own emotions, I can meet others at their place of need and concern.[2]

The words quoted above from Hebrews 5:12 certainly support emotional health as a sign of spiritual maturity. So where are your worship ministry participants in this progression toward spiritual and emotional maturity? As one minister of discipleship used to tell me, "Most of our church members don't have 40 years of Christian teaching under their belt, instead they've only had one year of Christian teaching 40 times!"

So I ask you, what are you doing in your church and worship ministry to grow disciples? The answers I usually hear are: "We have a great worship service and some Bible study groups," or "We have something going on every night of the week for our members," or "I make sure to include a devotional in our weekly rehearsal." But are we growing disciples? Presenting endless studies that are information-driven are not working. Our declining statistics and increasing incidence of church conflict prove that fact. Contemporary cell group churches often have significantly less than half of their worship service attendance involved in small groups. And traditional churches have lots of activity, but very little measurable discipleship to show for it. We must fall before our holy God and offer completely surrendered lives. Then we must rise to the mission of making disciples.

What is the solution? What process will intentionally and measurably build worshiping disciples on mission with God? It is obvious that much of what we are doing now in church is not working to that end. Relying solely on singing and preaching for an hour a week will not build transformed disciples of our Lord. Neither will weekly classes taught by untrained lay teachers or videos presented to passive listeners. Later in this book, I will present a discipleship plan designed to grow disciples who are ready to be

2. Scazzero and Bird, *The Emotionally Healthy Church*, 66.

sent on mission. Then we will lay out a process for sending them on mission. Let's take a look at how Jesus sent his disciples on mission.

> These were his (Jesus') instructions: "Take nothing for the journey except a staff—no bread, no bag, no money in your belts. Wear sandals but not an extra tunic. Whenever you enter a house, stay there until you leave that town. And if any place will not welcome you or listen to you, shake the dust off your feet when you leave, as a testimony against them." They went out and preached that people should repent. They drove out many demons and anointed many sick people with oil and healed them. Mark 6:8–13, NIV

Jesus, the son of God, walked this earth where we live. He chose followers and called them one by one to join him. Immediately, Jesus began teaching them about the kingdom of God and their place in it. They saw the glory of God in Jesus' miracles and were presented with the process of discipleship.

Then something unusual happened. Jesus sent His followers out on mission. It's amazing. Why would Jesus do such a thing with newly recruited followers who were so green with inexperience? Had they seen everything Christ could do? No. Had they learned everything he had to teach them? No. Had they seen enough to become missionaries? Yes! So, Jesus gave them power and authority, and he sent them to preach and heal. He sent them on mission. The circle of missional living had begun.

Can you imagine how they felt? Were they scared? Or were they naïve, bolstered by false security and eager to "take on the world"? Whatever their feelings, the bottom line is that they responded with obedience. And that is exactly how God expects us to respond.

It was risky for Jesus to send his disciples out so early in their ministry. But Jesus sent them anyway. Going on mission is the hammer and heat through which a disciple is forged. If our spirit must be like purified silver to reflect God, our will must be like iron to confront the world with the Gospel. The strength of a disciple's will is forged on mission as we take Christ to the world. And when we come back to worship, our worship will mean more than it ever has. We will have seen and known the power of God in ways we can never experience sitting in a church building. Our experience on mission will impact the depth of our worship time and again.

Ed Stetzer, master of missional wordplay, says that church members think their calling is to "pay, pray, and get out of the way so the professional staff can have their say." We teach our people "passivity, rather than activity." Those who "spend no time rowing the boat have too much time to rock the boat."[3] The truth is that spectators in the mission of Christ to win the world will almost always be emotional infants. The famous Baptist preacher from London's Metropolitan Tabernacle, Charles H. Spurgeon, once said, "Every Christian is either a missionary or an impostor."[4] Real worship and true discipleship will not allow us to be spectators to the mission of God. God is calling each of us into the circle of missional living.

It's a challenge to mobilize our churches to go on mission. But being on mission is absolutely crucial to experiencing the circle of missional living. The church that remains secure inside the church building is like the man who jumped off a 100-story building. As he passed the 40th floor in his rapid descent, he was heard shouting "So far, so good." Things may seem fine now, but there is a crash coming.

Why don't we as worship leaders move people beyond sitting and watching? Why do we seem powerless to confront and lead our people to missional discipleship? Are we dysfunctional leaders enabling a dysfunctional membership to remain spiritual babies? Do we set ourselves above them as a privileged class of priests, doing the work for them so they remain indebted to us? If we do not lead our members through the circle of missional living they will remain emotional infants. Do you enjoy leading a worship team that acts like a kindergarten class? I don't. The circle of missional living beckons us to something far greater—growing worshiping disciples on mission for Christ.

Return to the Cross

In the Jewish Temple there was an inner room called the holy of holies. The holy of holies was kept private by a heavy curtain. Only Jewish priests of highest standing were allowed to enter and commune with God behind the veil. But Jesus' death for us removed the veil from God's presence. At the exact moment Christ died for each of us, the curtain was torn open by a heavenly force. God's presence is accessible to all, his face forever unveiled. Through faith in Christ we become priests of highest standing. In him we enter the presence of God.

3. Stetzer, Great Commission Resurgence Video Conference, White Oak Conference Center, S.C., 2011.

4. Spurgeon, "A Sermon and Reminiscence."

"Man of sorrows" what a name
For the son of God who came
Ruined sinners to reclaim!
Hallelujah, what a Savior!

Christ in you is the only hope of glory. No program or event, no institution or club, no style or format, can give you his glory. The circle of missional living flows from the holy of holies right through that torn curtain into our worship, discipleship, and mission. If there is to be eternal glory in this life, it comes through the risen Christ. His glory is activated by the presence of the Holy Spirit in us and flows back to the Father in a glorious circle. Are you willing to let him take you full circle?

Bearing shame and scoffing rude,
In my place condemned he stood,
Sealed my pardon with his blood;
Hallelujah, what a Savior!

What curtain has veiled God's glory for you? What curtain is hiding his face from you? What curtain has bound his embrace of you? Step into the circle of missional living. Know God's glory. Hallelujah!

Guilty, vile, and helpless we;
Spotless Lamb of God was he;
Full atonement, can it be?
Hallelujah, what a Savior!

Questions for Thought and Discussion

With Paul as your example, examine your own personal worship. If you put your own worship beside Paul's expression of worship, how would you evaluate the depth and expression of your own worship?

With Paul as your example, examine your own discipleship. If you put your own discipleship beside Paul's definition of discipleship, how would you evaluate yours?

Have you compartmentalized worship, discipleship, and mission in your own life? How? What are some ways you can re-establish the circle of missional living with all three elements active in your life?

How can each element in the circle of worship-discipleship-mission strengthen and deepen each other in your daily life? What changes do you need to make in your life to enable the circle of missional living?

At what emotional level—infant, child, adolescent, adult—do you find yourself? What are the characteristics of the emotional level you exhibit in daily life, good and bad?

How would joining God on mission in your daily life help you grow as an emotionally mature disciple?

Are there any veils over your heart keeping you from entering into the presence of God? List them here. Pray for God to tear them open for his glory.

7

The Circle of Worship: A Vertical Vortex

When a Samaritan woman came to draw water, Jesus said to her, "Will you give me a drink?" (His disciples had gone into the town to buy food.)

The Samaritan woman said to him, "You are a Jew and I am a Samaritan woman. How can you ask me for a drink?" (For Jews do not associate with Samaritans.)

Jesus answered her, "If you knew the gift of God and who it is that asks you for a drink, you would have asked him and he would have given you living water."

"Sir," the woman said, "you have nothing to draw with and the well is deep. Where can you get this living water? Are you greater than our father Jacob, who gave us the well and drank from it himself, as did also his sons and his flocks and herds?"

Jesus answered, "Everyone who drinks this water will be thirsty again, but whoever drinks the water I give him will never thirst. Indeed, the water I give him will become in him a spring of water welling up to eternal life."

The woman said to him, "Sir, give me this water so that I won't get thirsty and have to keep coming here to draw water."

> He told her, "Go, call your husband and come back."
>
> "I have no husband," she replied.
>
> Jesus said to her, "You are right when you say you have no husband. The fact is, you have had five husbands, and the man you now have is not your husband. What you have just said is quite true."
>
> "Sir," the woman said, "I can see that you are a prophet. Our fathers worshiped on this mountain, but you Jews claim that the place where we must worship is in Jerusalem."
>
> Jesus declared, "Believe me, woman, a time is coming when you will worship the Father neither on this mountain nor in Jerusalem. You Samaritans worship what you do not know; we worship what we do know, for salvation is from the Jews. Yet a time is coming and has now come when the true worshipers will worship the Father in spirit and truth, for they are the kind of worshipers the Father seeks. God is spirit, and his worshipers must worship in spirit and in truth."
>
> The woman said, "I know that Messiah" (called Christ) "is coming. When he comes, he will explain everything to us."
>
> Then Jesus declared, "I who speak to you am he."
> John 4:7-26, NIV

When I take a bowl of water and begin to stir it slowly with a large spoon, the water will begin to swirl. The energy from my hand powering the spoon transfers to the water. As I increase the speed of the spoon, the water swirls faster. A vortex occurs in the center of the bowl where everything is drawn forward, inward, and downward simultaneously. If I have filled the bowl to the brim with water, the vortex will send the water out over the edge to soak the table around it.

This is a picture of the worship vortex. God fills the bowl of his church with the living water of Christ. He stirs the water with his mighty hand. His instrument to stir the living water is spirit and truth. Spirit and truth propel our worship forward, inward, and outward simultaneously. The worship vortex draws everything to Christ at the center, then propels us out of the church to soak everything around us with the gospel. The worship vortex is the ignition key for personal discipleship and mission in the life of a Christian.

Mike Glenn, preaching for LifeWay Worship Week in the summer of 2011, shared the vortex analogy. His worship team at Brentwood Baptist Church, Nashville, Tenn., uses the term "vertical vortex" for the worship experiences they hope to enable for their church. A vortex is something regarded as drawing into its powerful current everything that surrounds it. As I said earlier, Jesus gave the ultimate worship formula in John 12:32 when he said, "If I be lifted up, I will draw all to me." He is the vortex of the universe. When we worship in spirit and truth, the vortex of Christ's saving power draws all to him.

Jesus was passing through Samaria with his disciples. At midday they passed Jacob's well. He instructed his disciples to go into town so he could talk to a woman who had come to draw water from the well. She was at the well in the hottest part of the day to avoid contact with her neighbors. Jesus looked into her life and told her the sin he saw there. She immediately tried to distract him with something controversial—worship. Her question might read like this in today's language: "My people worship on Mount Gerizim. Our worship is contemporary and appeals to the senses. Your people worship at Jerusalem. Your worship is traditional and orderly, appealing to the mind. Which is right?"

Her tactic should be very familiar to us. Jesus is looking deep into our hearts to identify sin, but we are picking fights about worship style: "Your people like orderly traditional worship, but my people like exciting contemporary worship." Does that sound familiar? Starting a worship war is a devious way to deflect attention when Jesus starts convicting us of our sin. We do it all the time.

But Jesus countered the woman's question with a simple yet profound statement: "A time is coming and has now come when the true worshipers will worship the Father in spirit and truth" (John 4:23, NIV). Jesus' arrival on earth was the sunrise for a new era of worship dawning on mankind. The full sunlight would not be revealed until Jesus' mission was complete.

First, worship would become fully empowered by Christ's sacrificial death and victorious resurrection—the gospel. Second, worship would be fully consummated by the gift of God's Spirit. When these two epic events were fulfilled, worship was no longer contained in temples. Worship is now expressed through the lives of disciples who drink the water of life. We become God's temple. God's spirit has replaced sensationalism, and the truth of the gospel has replaced traditionalism.

Where can we find the most basic model of worship in spirit and truth? Come to the dark pathways in oppressive places where believers wear black and slip through the night to small, dimly-lit rooms. There, they worship, pray, and study the Bible. They are outlaws because of their faith in Christ. They could be arrested and killed at any minute; yet they live to follow Jesus. These courageous believers are multiplying disciples at an astounding rate. They are winning others to Christ, training them, and sending them out faster than church growth experts can comprehend. How are they doing such amazing things under such trying circumstances? What is their source of power? They dare to believe that the work of Christ can be done with nothing more than his Word and his Spirit. Nothing has the power to ignite our lives as do God's Spirit and Truth.

We assume that pianos, guitars, drums, an organ, and a comfortable building equipped with the latest technology are required for real worship. We think we need to present a particular style of music with correct instrumentation and the best players. Yet Jesus tells us that spirit and truth empower real worship. God's Holy Spirit, the engine for true worship, is empowered by his Word. Throughout the Bible, we see the power of God's Word. When prophets spoke on behalf of God, people were healed or cursed, and nations arose and fell. When Jesus' disciples spoke, demons were banished and hearts were opened to salvation. John 1 states that God's Word became flesh in Jesus Christ and dwelt among us full of power and grace. Paul testified to the power of the gospel in Romans 1:16a (HCSB): "For I am not ashamed of the gospel, because it is God's power for salvation to everyone who believes."

The gospel is God's Word made flesh in Jesus. What is more powerful than the gospel of Jesus presented in Spirit and Truth? Absolutely nothing! It truly is a vortex that draws everything surrounding it into its powerful current.

> The third time he (Jesus) said to him,
> "Simon son of John, do you love me?"
> Peter was hurt because Jesus asked him the third time,
> "Do you love me?"
> He said, "Lord, you know all things; you know that I love you."
> Jesus said, "Feed my sheep." John 21:17, NIV

This statement led to an important revelation for me. My calling as a worship leader is to help people fall in love with God. Almost 25 years ago, I heard Ken Hemphill say, "Most issues of church growth resolve themselves when church members fall deeply in love with God." This statement led to an important revelation for me. My calling as a worship leader is to help people fall in love with God. And I don't mean 'sentimental romantic' love, but 'surrender in total obedience' kind of love.

The vertical vortex of spirit and truth compels us to fall deeply in love with God. A deep love for God is at the heart of the circle of missional living. That love is demonstrated in worship through personal lifestyle and corporate acts. Worship is to Christian life what going on a date with your spouse is to marriage. The time spent together is a celebration and expression of total commitment. It reminds me that "I Only Have Eyes for You," as the pop song says. I express my own incompleteness and the need I have for my spouse. Our hearts affirm our growing unity in each other. These elements of a date with our spouse are present in authentic worship as well. Yet I continually see churches stop worshiping to sing a birthday song, make announcements, or talk about yesterday's sports event. This interrupts the energy driving the vortex, like taking a phone call in the middle of a dinner date with your spouse.

In his book *Sacred Pathways: Discover Your Soul's Path to God,* Gary Thomas wrote: "When I die, I hope that I will have been able to love God with everything I am: I will have worked to turn my mind over to his wisdom and truth, my hands over to his service, my sight over to his beauty, and my entire being over to enjoying his presence."[1]

Jesus called his disciples to share the gospel with the world. Why were these men chosen for such an important task? The four gospels present a clear picture of them in their weakness and humanity. We see their lack of spiritual perception; we know their naïve ambition; we empathize with their fears and doubts. The truth is that they were a lot like you and me. Yet God worked through them to change the world, and he is ready to work through us too. The disciples had encountered the resurrected Christ and fallen deeply in love with God. Worship in spirit and truth produces such love.

> But I enter Your house by the abundance of Your faithful love;
> I bow down toward Your holy temple in reverential awe of You. Psalm 5:7, HCSB

How can worship leaders enable others to fall deeply in love with God? Here are eight principles that can empower corporate worship as a vertical vortex of spirit and truth each time you assemble as the church:

1. Thomas, *Sacred Pathways: Discover Your Soul's Path to God,* 68.

1. Gather God's family. Whatever your worship tradition or style, liturgical or free, we must allow our people to re-establish their identity as God's family, either through fellowship or liturgy. Whether with greetings and laughter, or through meditation with quiet music, we become once again a family gathered to worship our Father. Embrace the joy, love, and acceptance of being family. Cultivate and maintain that closeness throughout the worship gathering. Worship leaders can express the warmth and joy of encouragement and love in their words, tone of voice, and posture.
2. Proclaim and celebrate God's revelation. Begin the service with a powerful proclamation that reveals who God is and what he is doing in the world. Throughout the Bible, God bursts into our mundane lives to announce his power and presence. Refuse to let your worship service get off to a "lame" start. Powerfully celebrate God's coming to us.
3. Include the Biblical elements of worship through revelation and response. Isaiah 6 models God's revelation and our response. Build drama and flow throughout worship by reenacting revelation and response. Then analyze carefully your weekly worship to make sure it includes each of these four Biblical elements: God gathers His family; God reminds us of his mighty acts and the gift of Christ; We respond to God's love in Christ through praise, confession, repentance, and surrender; and God sends us out as his missionaries to our world. These four elements do not have to be compartmentalized into sections. Allow them to flow freely and be repeated as needed within the worship gathering. Create dramatic flow throughout to facilitate the powerful portrayal of the gospel.
4. Focus totally on God and the gospel throughout the service. Teach and remind worshipers constantly that God first revealed himself in love. Our response should be surrendering all we are and have, not demanding something for ourselves. Encourage your worshipers continually to sing to God and not just about God. Help them understand the necessity of engaging intentionally with God every minute during worship. Can they hear his voice speaking directly to them in the songs, the Scripture readings, prayers, sermon, and other expressions? Are they responding in confession, repentance, and surrender? Make a date with God to connect with him in every service. Analyze your worship to see if there are distractions or interruptions to the vertical

vortex. Technical system checks are a must to make sure sound, video, lights, etc do not become a distraction.

5. Celebrate God transforming lives instead of promoting your church. Turn church stories into God stories. Help church members fall deeply in love with God rather than with you and your church. If they see God at work in your church, your church will be attractive without having to be attractional.
6. Promote participation. Avoid "performance mode" and "spectatorism." Creatively include Scripture, prayer, and testimony led by many different worship participants. Including choirs to facilitate congregational worship will get more people participating regardless of your musical style. Do reach for excellence as an extravagant gift to God, our unblemished lamb given in sacrifice.
7. Discover resources to best convey the message to a modern congregation in their cultural context. Study the demographics of your community and determine what your church members are reading and listening to in their daily lives. Poll your congregation to discover their heart languages. Then intentionally design worship in their heart language to connect them with God, his kingdom, and his mission.
8. Send them out: Place announcements and recognitions at the close of worship to avoid interrupting the focus on God. They will remember best the last thing they hear. Include no more than three announcements and be sure they apply to the whole church. Finally, commission them to be "the church" in the world, actively joining God on mission where he has placed you every day. Transform the benediction into a commissioning. Say something to this effect: "We are God's people, let's go live like it!" or "God has been revealed to us today; let's respond by joining him on mission every day this week."

We must understand that while God uses the elements of worship, he is not the elements of worship. We must not mistake our worship activity for God. No single methodology holds the key to unlocking powerful worship. Again, Christ-powered worship happens when the power of God's spirit is present and unhindered and God's word of truth, the gospel message, is presented in all its power. Regardless of whether our favorite form of worship is contemporary or traditional, free or liturgical, if we do not find the power of God's spirit and truth, it will all be an empty show.

In summary, here are my ten commandments for worship leaders:

1. Thou shalt have no other worship gods before me

The first of God's Ten Commandments makes it clear that worship is all about God and not about us. Neither is it about style or format. If we put anything on the worship throne in place of God, he calls it idolatry. Lead your church to bring him their all, every time, in every service. Anything else is self-worship.

2. Thou shalt never take your people where you have not been

Be a worshiper every day yourself. Fall deeply in love with God. Worship means showing in every action and attitude the ultimate worth of God. Showing his worth must be our aim 24/7, not just an hour on Sunday. When you crave God's presence every moment of every day, he will show you amazing things and take you to amazing places. A worship leader must live full circle in worship, discipleship and mission every day.

3. Thou shalt focus worship on God

Point to God in everything you say and do in worship. Lead your church to sing to him, not just about him. Use Scripture in spoken intros or testify to God's power—not yesterday's sports event, someone's birthday, or any other distraction. Move the announcements to the end of the service. Maintain a dramatic flow that moves people through the redemption story: God reveals his glory then we respond in repentance, trust, and obedience (Isaiah 6). Don't interrupt the vortex of total focus on almighty God.

4. Thou shalt call forth the called and gifted

Every member of your team should have a calling from God to be a worshiper and a worship leader. Don't sacrifice the team for that one who is absent from rehearsal or often arrives late. To be called by God is to be compelled by the Holy Spirit to give him our very best at all times. Just as important as calling, every team member must be God-gifted with artistic talent. Excellence in our artistic craft is our worthy sacrifice to God. Building an effective team of musicians, artists, tech, and support is like working a puzzle (Ephesians 4). Forcing a piece into the wrong place will ruin the whole picture.

5. Honor thy authority structure

God has placed those in authority over us to work his will in our lives. Usually our authority is the senior pastor, but our authority could be another person or team designated by the church. Regardless of who fills this role—or their background, leadership style, and personal tastes—God is calling you to be subject to that person's authority. Communicate, cooperate, be teachable, and open with this leader as he/she works to lead you and your team. Serve this person in return.

6. Love thy team as thyself

Jesus told his followers that the first shall be last, the greatest will be the least (Matt. 20:16). We are most like Christ when we are sharing grace with someone who doesn't deserve it. Be graceful as you hold your team accountable. Always communicate personal issues face to face (Matt. 18:15–16). Follow an intentional process to disciple your worship team into deeper devotion to God. Jesus showed us that we must do this in the context of relationship. You cannot make withdrawals from someone's "account" until you have invested in that person. Involve your team, too, in planning and feedback to capitalize on their creativity.

7. Honor the heart languages of thy church

We would all like to have one service full of spiritually mature believers who could truly worship in any style. But that won't happen until heaven. In this life, we are wired by God to relate and communicate in languages. Styles arise from the variety of artistic languages used within cultures. Heart language is our most meaningful tool from God to connect people with him. The more effectively we connect Christians with God, the more effectively we can move them to discipleship and mission. A good worship leader researches and discovers the heart languages (music, drama, visual art, artistic expression, language, etc.) that best connect their church with God. It doesn't have to be just contemporary and traditional music. Gospel, country, pop, urban, jazz, world, adult contemporary, sacred, classical, bluegrass—they are all styles that can be used to connect your church with God. Teach to a visual generation using outlines and props. Also use video, drama, creative movement, puppetry, mime, dance, visual art, pottery, and all the other artistic forms God gave to honor him. So don't close your eyes—literally or figuratively. Be sure to watch your congregation during worship to see if your worship style is connecting them to God. Get feedback from others and evaluate constantly.

8. Thou shalt not perform

True worship is participation, not performance. If the congregation is no more than spectators, true worship is not happening. Provide participation for as many as possible, not just the platform leaders. Involve choirs, Scripture readers, prayer leaders, guided prayer, testimonies, creative arts groups, ushers, greeters, etc. of all ages and ethnicities. Choose keys for congregational song that are singable by the average person. Staying within the range of Bb below middle C to high Eb will work as a rule of thumb. Adapt the key of radio songs for congregational use by these guidelines. And remember, Jesus' formula for worship is simple: "If I be lifted up, I will draw all to me." The world can see an entertaining performance anywhere, but we offer eternal life in Christ. Make it all about him and get out of the way.

9. Thou shalt eliminate distractions

Plan and rehearse well to avoid sound system problems, sudden lighting changes, sound system feedback, awkward song transitions, etc. Pay attention to the details. Video record the worship service and evaluate as a team your onstage motions, facial expression, entrances and exits, attention during prayers, etc. Our right to personal expression is subject to God's calling to connect and lead his people to him. Be careful to match your personal onstage fashion to the style of the majority of the congregation. Paul wrote: "I have become all things to all men so that by all possible means I might save some" (1 Cor. 9:22, NIV).

10. Go ye therefore

Worship should ignite the church to discipleship and mission. If we hoard our God-given giftedness inside the church, we ignore God's call to join him on mission to redeem the world. Organize and empower your worship ministry to go into your community on a regular basis to build witnessing relationships. Our goal is this: Every member a missionary!

Since God created worship for himself, every element of worship must focus on him. Release the vertical vortex to move worship beyond "business as usual," from a sink full of lukewarm water into a vortex of centrifugal force, from a partly cloudy day into a funnel cloud of awesome power. Worship in spirit and truth leads us to fall in love with God. When we love God, we will love others. Ignited by his spirit we share his word of truth with them every day on mission. Do you love him? Feed his sheep!

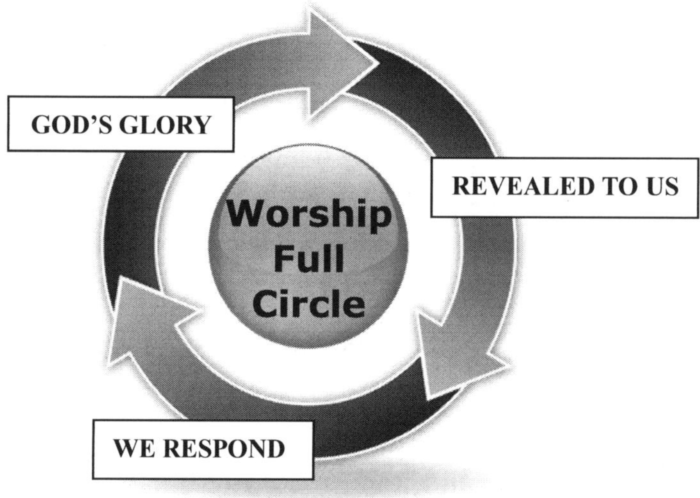

Diagram 2

Return to the Cross

Amazing grace! how sweet the sound,
That saved a wretch like me!
I once was lost, but now am found,
Was blind, but now I see.[2]

The distant image of three people drifts through my mind: a Samaritan woman, a slave ship captain, and a college student. The woman was blind to her destructive circle of self-abuse called adultery. The captain was blind to his own enslavement to money made from human cargo. The college student was blind to the addictions sneaking through the back entrance of life.

2. Newton, "Amazing Grace! How Sweet the Sound," Public Domain.

Thro' many dangers, toils, and snares,
I have already come;
'Tis grace hath bro't me safe thus far,
And grace will lead me home.

Unknown to them, Christ had set an appointment with each of the three. Jesus looks into their eyes and hearts, revealing the dangers, toils, and snares he sees deep inside. With incredible grace, he offers unconditional love. The snare is crushed and his children come home to him forever.

When we've been there ten thousand years,
Bright shining as the sun,
We've no less days to sing God's praise
Than when we first begun.

The Samaritan woman runs to her village. "Come see the man who told me everything I have ever done," she shouts graciously to those who had no grace for her. John Newton, the slave ship captain, abandons ship to write the most poignant and popular lyric of grace in the history of the world, "Amazing Grace." As a college student, face-down on my den floor, I receive grace and fall deeply in love with God. The song of grace continues to be written at the cross. Let the song fill your life too.

Questions for Thought and Discussion

What must change in your church's worship service to unleash the vertical vortex of focus on God?

What are the obstacles in your church to focusing totally on God in worship? What are the obstacles in your own attitude to total focus on God in worship?

How will you lead those in your circle of influence to experience the worship vortex in your church?

How will you know if you are making progress in this commitment? How will you know if you are not achieving positive results?

Describe what it would be like if your church were to truly worship in spirit and truth.

8

The Circle of Discipleship: God's Parenting Process

> But the fruit of the Spirit is love, joy, peace, patience, kindness, goodness, faith, gentleness, self-control. Galatians 5:22-23, HCSB

WHAT ARE THE CHARACTERISTICS God looks for in a mature disciple? We want to make it complicated, but it really is very simple. The fruit of the Spirit produced in our lives is the evidence of true discipleship: love, joy, peace, patience, kindness, goodness, faith, gentleness, and self-control. These characteristics can only be produced by total surrender to God. We cannot manufacture them ourselves. They are the fruit of *shachach* and *proskuneo*, falling before God every day in total submission.

Discipleship is the ongoing process of maturing as a child of the Father. He calls us into relationship by the power of the cross. He leads us into discipleship through the presence of the Spirit. He grows us into spiritual maturity as the Spirit applies his Word to our lives. Discipleship is a process empowered by spirit and truth. The Bible calls it sanctification—being set apart and re-made as God's own. "I am sure of this, that He who started a good work in you will carry it on to completion until the day of Christ Jesus" (Phil. 1:6, HCSB).

In chapter six, I cited *The Emotionally Healthy Church* by Pete Scazzero and Warren Bird to identify the levels of Christian spiritual maturity from infant to adult. How can God take an immature and selfish spiritual child like me and recreate me in his image? As a loving earthly father raises his children, so our loving heavenly Father raises us spiritually. Through this love relationship, he nurtures us toward trust and obedience. Affection, discipline, teaching, and accountability all flow from that relationship. God, our Father, has appointed his Word as our textbook and the Holy Spirit as our tutor in this process. In chapter five of Matthew, Jesus gathered his new followers to teach the parenting process our Father uses to raise his children to spiritual maturity. God's goal is to mature us to the point where we can inherit the family business—his mission of redemption.

> When he saw the crowds, he went up on the mountain, and after he sat down, his disciples came to him. Matthew 5:1, NASB.

In Matthew 5:1–14 we find Jesus' earliest teaching on the transforming process through which our Father grows disciples. This teaching is commonly known as the Beatitudes because the Latin word for blessing is *beatus*. The Beatitudes, the opening section of Jesus' Sermon on the Mount, are a pronouncement of blessing upon those who seek him. But Jesus' words also challenged the very core of Judaism, the traditional religion of his day.

Jesus' followers had only recently responded to his call to follow. They had watched his first miracles and had seen the crowds run to him, yet they were spiritual newborns in many ways. They were people like us trying to find the way to real meaning in life. Now Jesus gathered them to teach the life-process through which God grows us to spiritual maturity. This process mirrors 1 Peter 2:2 (HCSB): "Like newborn infants, desire the unadulterated spiritual milk, so that you may grow by it in your salvation." The reward for submitting to God's parenting is being blessed by him. Blessing includes happiness but goes deeper. Blessedness comes from knowing God's peace and presence at the deepest level. True disciples live a lifestyle of worship and are blessed with an unshakable awareness of our Father's presence, even in the hardest times.

> He opened his mouth and began to teach them, saying: "Blessed are the poor in spirit, for theirs is the kingdom of heaven." Matthew 5:2–3, NASB

God created us for eternal significance, but we are born into this world with nothing except what he has given. We have nothing to offer our Heavenly Father that did not first come from him. But "God is love" (1 John 4:8, HCSB). Despite our poverty of spirit, he is a perfect parent and loves us to the fullest extent possible. Nothing we can do can earn more love since he loves us completely already. Yet we are born into this world with a sinful nature leading us to believe we are the center of the universe. A newborn demands instant gratification. A spiritual baby thinks everything should revolve around him or her. To take our first step to God, we must confess that we are spiritually impoverished.

We must not dare think that God's process for growing disciples is a self-help program. It is far more radical than that. This first step means death to our sinful pride. Poor in spirit is not a state of depression but a place where our self-reliance is broken. Being broken by God hurts, but it is a hurt that leads to being re-made in our Father's image. We must clearly see our sin through God's eyes and repent of that sin. There is no way around it. Repentance is not just being sorry, it is being sorry enough to die to self and quit the sin. This first step came at the greatest cost to God—he gave his Son. God took your debt and paid it forever at the cross. And because of that, the kingdom of heaven is yours if you come to Christ as Savior.

> Blessed are those who mourn, because they shall be comforted. Matthew 5:4, NASB

Mourning is the cry of a spiritual newborn drawing first breath in God's world. Before we are reborn we live in sin, like a womb where everything exists for us alone. Then we are born into God's kingdom, and we cry out in shock that we are no longer the center of everything. But our heavenly Father pulls us to his chest to embrace his newborn child. He lifts us up, wipes our tears, and assures us of his loving presence. Then he begins to feed us and help us walk toward spiritual growth. He comforts us when we are overwhelmed by this big world with its many unknowns. God cannot comfort those who are unwilling to mourn.

Learning to obey the heavenly Father is an ongoing process for his children. Every day we must offer our stubborn will to him again. There will be tears of mourning when we fall or when we are disciplined. And in those times, instead of demanding "God, get me out of this," we must ask, "God, what can I get out of this? What will you teach me from this?" The comfort of God's presence enables our obedience and trust. He is growing us in discipleship to send us on mission.

> Blessed are the gentle, for they shall inherit the earth. Matthew 5:5, NASB

Children go to kindergarten to learn to share their toys, play with others, and obey their teachers. They learn not to hit other children or pitch tantrums. God teaches us gentleness as we learn to depend on him and love others as ourselves. He calls it his great commandment. Total dependence on our Father produces a gentle approach to life. He is growing the heart of a disciple who can love others as he loves us. Those who share gentleness with others are heirs to God's kingdom.

Of course, the world does not see it that way. The world adores those who are brash and loud. But the gentle are adored by those who know them best. Gentleness does not mean we are forbidden to express strong feelings. But a gentle response to life should replace volatile reaction for a maturing child of God. That kind of gentleness springs from the assurance of God's presence, and it frees us from the need to response to every threat—real or perceived.

> Blessed are those who hunger and thirst for righteousness,
> for they shall be satisfied. Matthew 5:6, NASB

For a child of God who has experienced grace, gentleness is only the beginning. Now we have grown past the spiritual infant stage into childhood. As we grow, we truly hunger and thirst for a right relationship with our Father. An unquenchable hunger drives us to feel our Father's hug and see his smile. Disobedience then is disloyalty to the love relationship that we are building.

As God's children, our relationship is far more than following rules and regulations. Instead, through the Spirit, God himself lives inside us and works his way from the inside out. The Holy Spirit, active in us, enables us to live a righteous life as a response to God's love. The whisper of God calls us, "I love those who love me; and those who seek me, (will) find me" (Prov. 8:17, NIV). The disciple will grow from spiritual infant thirsting for milk and comfort, to child of God hungering to learn of him in mutual love and trust.

> Blessed are the merciful, for they shall receive mercy.
> Matthew 5:7, NASB

As we move into older childhood in God's school of spiritual maturity, the challenges get tougher. Life itself and the people in it can be very annoying. But God's eyes are eyes of mercy. A growing child of God will see others through his eyes. Things that bring tears to his eyes bring tears to ours. A disciple learns to look, feel, and respond with mercy. The characteristic that began as gentleness matures into mercy. Mercy is a must if we have any hope of being effective on mission.

Just a few minutes after this teaching, Jesus told those assembled: "For if you forgive people their wrongdoing, your heavenly Father will forgive you as well. But if you don't forgive people, your Father will not forgive your wrongdoing" (Matt. 6:14–15, HCSB). Mercy prevails at the judgment seat of God. Mercy must prevail in daily discipleship. My pastor, Ed Carney, at Riverland Hills Baptist Church in Columbia, S.C., says of Jesus' statement, "Do you think Jesus is fooling around when he says if we don't forgive others God will not forgive us? Is he joking? No! He means exactly what he says: Forgive everybody, everything, every time."

> Blessed are the pure in heart, for they shall see God.
> Matthew 5:8, NASB

Parents hope and pray that their teenagers will remain pure. A commitment to purity is crucial to every child of God. To resist the temptations of the world, we must trust implicitly that God is the only source for our every need. This trust level requires that we see God at work in every aspect of life. We find him there at every step. Our all-knowing Father is never surprised by the circumstances in which we find ourselves. Knowing this we begin to take life's challenges in stride—his stride.

But purification is ongoing. Because the world is a battlefield between Satan and God, life is a battle between godliness and godlessness. Sanctification requires hand-to-hand combat with our sin. No doubt, God is our comforting Father throughout the daily battles. But he is also a strong Father who expects obedience. Being superficially religious won't cut it, no matter how impressive we seem. He wants to purify us so we see him clearly in every moment of every day. If we're going to join God on mission, it's crucial to see clearly where he is at work. Purity, then, is a single-minded focus on seeing God and remaining untainted by the filth we see around us.

> Blessed are the peacemakers, for they shall be called sons of God. Matthew 5:9, NASB

When God fills his disciples with mercy and purity, inner peace moves in. Spiritually mature disciples who have found God's calling for their lives possess that peace. The Jewish people bestow the hope of peace on others with the blessing *shalom*. Shalom is a one-word prayer for the restoration of the world to God's design. A mature disciple possesses the personal peace of knowing God's design and then partnering with him to restore that design to the world.

Peacemakers bring calm to a raging world. But they are not naïve. Soon after his Sermon on the Mount, Jesus sent his disciples out into the world. "Look, I'm sending you out like sheep among wolves. Therefore be as shrewd as serpents and as harmless as doves," he told them in Matthew 10:16 (HCSB). Peacemaking requires remarkable inner strength. Every attitude Jesus has presented in the discipleship process to this point will be required of a peacemaker on mission. Peacemakers are spiritual adults capable of raising spiritual children in God's family. They have died to self and experienced brokenness and mourning. The kingdom of heaven has become theirs by accepting Christ's death in their place. They receive God's comfort and become gentle in the experience. A peacemaker is filled every day by a right relationship with God. Mercy and purity grow out of a peacemaker's life wherever they join God on mission.

A world at war with God cries out for peacemakers. God sends them on mission to birth people in Christ and raise them as disciples. They are acclaimed as sons of God, his grown children. Ah, the pinnacle of discipleship is attained. The mature disciple can now relax and enjoy the blessings, right? Wrong! Keep reading.

> Blessed are those who have been persecuted for the sake of righteousness, for theirs is the kingdom of heaven. Blessed are you when people insult you and persecute you, and falsely say all kinds of evil against you because of Me. Rejoice and be glad, for your reward in heaven is great; for in the same way they persecuted the prophets who were before you. Matthew 5:10–12, NASB

Just a short while after presenting the Beatitudes, Jesus prayed to his Father, "Your kingdom come, your will be done on earth as it is in heaven" (Matt. 6:10, KJV). Ever since the fall of man into sin, God has chosen to suspend his perfect will on earth so we might have the privilege of choosing him. God's perfect will is done in heaven, and he allows Satan to reign in hell. Earth is their battleground. The disciple lives on the battleground, and the world is at war. A disciple on mission must understand this truth.

The world hates godliness even as it hungers for God. Paul said to the citizens of Philippi, "Many live as enemies of the cross of Christ. Their destiny is destruction, their god is their stomach, and their glory is in their shame. Their mind is on earthly things" (Phil. 3:18–19, NIV). Earthly life is torn apart by this conflict.

Look at the modern media for proof. They exalt celebrities as gods of society, and we keep buying it. Then we tear those celebrities down at the first sign of human frailty, only to lift them up again when we crave more entertainment. During Jesus' last week in Jerusalem the crowds shouted,

"Hosanna," as he arrived, then cried, "Crucify him," five days later. As Christ-followers, the world will do that to us, too. The world yearns to possess what God has given us. But upon hearing what it will cost, they turn back to their pursuit of pleasure. Their lives are consumed with satisfying the lower instincts rather than lifting hearts and minds to God. The very ones who cry for our help turn against us.

When the world is against us, the Father's love endures. The kingdom of heaven is ours. Hallelujah! The forces of evil may take every earthly thing we own. They may even come for our lives. But they cannot steal our Father's ultimate gift. The souls of those who are in Christ will live forever with God. We are his children, and he is our Father. He has grown us to maturity, so now we move out with him to share the relationship with others. The discipleship process goes full circle.

> You are the salt of the earth; but if the salt has become tasteless, how can it be made salty again? It is no longer good for anything, except to be thrown out and trampled underfoot by men. Matthew 5:13, NASB

Those who heard Jesus teach that day could only begin to grasp the full meaning of what we call The Beatitudes. John MacArthur, in his book *The Jesus You Can't Ignore*, says: "The Sermon on the Mount was a critique of the Pharisees' religion. He condemned their doctrine; their phony approach to practical holiness; their pedantic style of Scripture twisting; and their smug overconfidence."[1] Do these charges apply to us today in the institutional church?

We see the Beatitudes from our vantage point this side of the cross. May our vantage point never de-sensitize us to God's parenting. Those who heard the Sermon on the Mount could hardly comprehend what this discipleship process would mean for them. They would be salt and light on mission to the world. Salt flavors, heals, and preserves. For us who would flavor the world for God, total dependence on him is essential. For us who would administer God's healing, self-sacrifice must reign. For we who would preserve the world for God, we must embrace daily repentance and purification. Otherwise, we become useless to him—flavoring without flavor, medicine without healing, preservative that rots. Uselessness should be a disciple's greatest fear!

1. MacArthur, *The Jesus You Can't Ignore*, 129.

> You are the light of the world. A city on a hill cannot be hidden. Matthew 5:14, NASB

What would you think of a marathon runner who loads his or her body with carbohydrates for the race and then sleeps in, misses the start, and spends the day watching the race on television? Too many of our church members are fat with God's nutrition yet never use it to fuel real work for the kingdom. "For though by this time you ought to be teachers, you need someone to teach you the basic principles of God's revelation. You need milk, not solid food," charged the writer of Hebrews (Heb. 5:12, HCSB).

Like worship, if discipleship is for our own enrichment alone, it becomes idolatry. Discipleship is the process of growing more Christ-like so that, like Christ, God can use us to reach people. He desires to use our relationship with him to bring others into relationship. Too often discipleship has been misinterpreted as "sit and savor." Jesus calls us to get up and go.

The apostle Paul exemplified going full circle in missional living. The ruthless persecutor of Christians encountered the living Christ face to face. Jesus' words to Paul on the Damascus road were the truth of the gospel. The word of truth took root in his heart, and he responded with brokenness. The power of the gospel gripped him, propelling him into the world. Paul was truly transformed. The cruelty and hardness of his own spirit gave way to the Holy Spirit. The ultimate Pharisee became the ultimate disciple. The ultimate disciple became the ultimate missionary. The ultimate missionary gave us the list of characteristics God expects from worshiping disciples on mission. Paul's life went full circle.

> The fruit of the Spirit is love, joy, peace, patience, kindness, goodness, faith, gentleness, self-control.
> Galatians 5:22–23,NASB

We have gone full circle in the process of discipleship. Are you submitting to our heavenly Father to grow you spiritually? Is the fruit of God's Spirit growing out of you? Are you partnering with God on mission to make disciples who make disciples? These are not goals we can attain, but rather the evidence of a life completely yielded to Christ in discipleship.

We must allow God, through the Holy Spirit, to produce his fruit in us. Without these spiritual traits active in our lives the world will reject us as hypocrites. If they see meanness, anger, harshness, anxiety, or lust in us, how can they embrace the God we claim has saved us from those things?

Go one step more. Think of the worship team that you lead. Do they produce the fruit of the Spirit, too? Do they show love, joy, peace, patience, kindness, goodness, faith, gentleness, and self-control in their daily lives? If not, you must partner with God to bring them into his process of parenting. Lead them into discipleship and take them on mission.

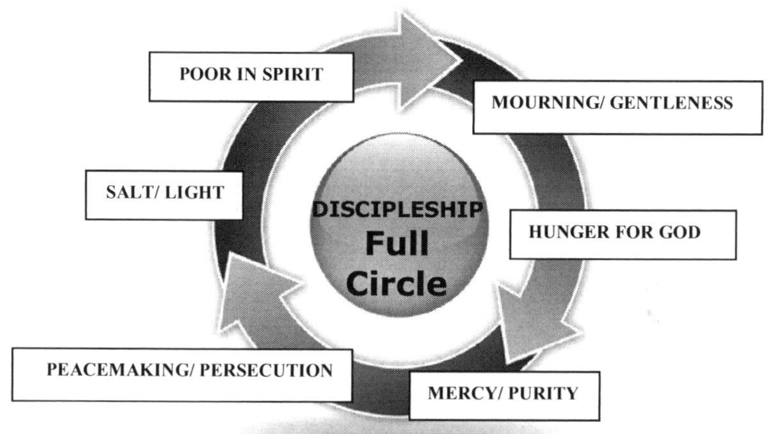

Diagram 3

Return to the Cross

Jesus, keep me near the cross. There a precious fountain,
Free to all a healing stream, flows from Calvary's mountain.
In the cross, in the cross be my glory ever,
Till my ransomed soul shall find rest beyond the river.[2]

Lord, I am under attack. I know this life is a battlefield between good and evil, but I am taking on enemy fire with no obvious route of escape. I confess that, in my panic, I can only cry out for you to send in air support or heavy artillery. But I hear your voice coming across the radio commanding me to hold my position. So teach me, Lord. Help me know how poor I am in spirit. Mourning my inability to save myself, I throw myself upon your mercy. Use this attack to bring me into a right relationship with you so that your Spirit may pour holiness out of my life in every situation.

2. Cross, "Jesus, Keep Me Near the Cross," Public Domain.

Near the cross! O Lamb of God, bring its scenes before me;
Help me walk from day to day with its shadow o'er me.
In the cross, in the cross be my glory ever,
Till my ransomed soul shall find rest beyond the river.

When your Son was on the cross for the sin of the world, he could have called for your rescue. But he remained in your will to his death. And from his death came life eternal. So, too, may the attacks of life produce your will in me. Lord, make me your disciple.

Questions for Thought and Discussion

Look at the Scripture for each of the Beatitudes in this chapter. List the primary quality from each verse that God wants to develop in your life.

Looking at your list above, put a checkmark at the point in the process to which you think you have progressed as a disciple. What characteristics are remaining for you to achieve?

Look at the fruit of the Spirit as listed above. List them here, and give yourself a letter grade for how well you exhibit these fruit in your own life. Now look at the list again and give your worship team a letter grade overall for how well they exhibit these qualities in their lives.

Is your worship team willing to invest the time and effort to grow in the circle of discipleship as expressed in the Beatitudes? Why or why not? What will it take for you to grow personally and then lead your team into deeper discipleship?

Remembering that this process must lead to the death of our self-centeredness, what are the main challenges facing your team? Facing you personally?

9

The Circle of Mission: From Attractional to Attractive Missional

> Forget the former things; do not dwell on the past. See, I am doing a new thing! Now it springs up; do you not perceive it? I am making a way in the wilderness and streams in the wasteland. Isaiah 43:18–19, NIV

God is on the move in the world today. He is constantly doing a new thing. New Testament scholars point out that the word "immediately" is used 41 times in the gospel of Mark. The use of such a dramatic word underscores the forward momentum of God's kingdom on earth.

In the last decade, a missional movement has begun among those who realize our church train is on the wrong track headed for a crash. Their prophetic cry implores the church to catch up with the new things God is doing. Fred Luter, New Orleans pastor and first African-American president of the Southern Baptist Convention, while insistent that the gospel remain unchanged, said, "We cannot expect to reach this do-rag, tattoo-wearing, ear-pierced, iPod, iPad, iPhone generation with an eight-track ministry. Things are changing and so we've got to some way, somehow change the methods of how we do things."[1]

Throughout this book, I have insisted that true worship ignites us to join God on his mission of redemption. The word "redeem" means to recover ownership by paying off a debt. The word "ignite" means to set afire.

1. Ledbetter, "Luter sees genuine open door for ethnic groups," June 20, 2012.

Worship in spirit and truth sets our hearts afire to join God in his mission to redeem the world.

Eric Alexander, Scottish pastor and theologian, speaking at the Urbana Missions Conference, supported this view:

> No Christian man or woman worshiping God and desiring his glory can be unmoved by the fact that there are areas of the world and nations where God is being robbed of his glory. That is why true worship and true mission always go together, and it is why the glory of God is the only ultimate missionary motive. There are, of course, others: compassion for the lost, obedience to the Great Commission and so on. But these are not the ultimate motive. The ultimate motive is the glory of God."[2]

In the early years of the missional movement, many of its main proponents took a dim view of corporate worship. Despite being effective missional prophets, they were still trying to comprehend worship in an attractional mindset. When I explain to people that discipleship and missions begin with worship, they often look at me in confusion. Their concept of worship is usually limited to an hour per week designed to attract the world to church. But God is on the move. It's time for us to move with him and get beyond the attractional methods that have held us back for so many years.

> A city built on a hill cannot be hidden.
> Neither do people light a lamp and put it under a bowl.
> Instead they put it on its stand,
> and it gives light to everyone in the house.
> Matthew 5:14b–16, NIV

As I drive through small towns or across the countryside, I enjoy reading church signs. Have you ever noticed how many church signs contain messages that present the singular message, "Come in"? A prominent billboard proclaims, "Let's meet at my house before the game this Sunday! Signed, God." Is the reader to think that the only way to find God is to go to a church on a Sunday? Service times, event promos, and slogans that push church attendance all show that our focus is inside the walls. Some signs assume the role of drive-by sniper as they attempt to put a 10-second guilt trip on us for not attending their church. I dream that one day I might see a church sign that simply says, "Do you have a need? Can we help you? Call us at 803–888–7777. We'll do our best to serve you."

2. Alexander, "True Worship and True Mission: For the Glory of God," speech at the Urbana Missions Conference, 1981.

It's true that Jesus used attractional methods to draw a crowd. And, from the crowd that followed Jesus, some became believers. But Jesus matured those believers through a distinct process of discipleship and missions. That process was never limited to sitting in the crowd as a spectator. Instead, God says, "Follow me," and "Go." Simply put, our call from God is to go make disciples who make disciples. Even though some will be won to Christ by coming to church, God's main strategy is for us to go to them.

Attractive missional worship focuses on growing worshiping disciples on mission. In contrast, attractional worship might be summarized as attracting people to church to serve Christ inside the church to attract more people into the church.

Again, God's primary strategy to win the world is to get his church into the world, not the world into churches.

> Jesus answered, "If you want to be perfect, go, sell your possessions and give to the poor, and you will have treasure in heaven. Then come, follow me" (Matt. 19:21, NIV.)

Have you heard of the mental illness of hoarding? People with this illness obtain massive amounts of possessions, jamming them into every space of their home until they have little room to live. When hoarded, possessions, which once had value and meaning, become rotten and useless. Are we spending our lives hoarding our gifts in the church while we ignore the call to pour out those gifts in our community on mission?

When the church trades mission for maintenance, members give up outside relationships and activities to spend their time and talents in church. When this happens new Christians lose the context among their non-believing friends where they can be on mission. And long-time members are kept so busy inside the church that no time remains to be on mission. Church budgets and expenditures also reveal if maintenance has overcome mission. God is calling us to shake the salt from the shaker and place the light of the gospel on the hilltop.

A friend of mine was serving as worship leader when his pastor resigned to go serve a mission church in Haiti. The worship leader remained with the church and resolved to lead his church to be more missional. When the church expanded his job description to include managing the church budget, he pronounced that the mission budget would no longer cover expenses for events presented on campus. Attractional events presented on campus would now be funded through program budgets. The mission budget was reserved for true mission projects presented in the community. Bravo!

Many of us are oblivious to God's call to be the gospel incarnate in our world.

God is calling his church to change the world. We cannot join God on his mission by staying inside the church building. Wake up, church! Something has to splash cold water in our faces and compel us to action. What will God use to stir us from slumber: an economic winter, another attack from an enemy, a natural disaster? Or will we simply be convicted by Christ's commission to redeem our communities for God?

> How then can they call on the one they have not believed in? And how can they believe in the one of whom they have not heard? And how can they hear without someone preaching to them? And how can they preach unless they are sent? Romans 10:14, NIV

Not all Christians are gifted to be evangelists, but all are called to be missionaries. We must develop a process to grow every church member into an effective missionary. Can you imagine the power and potential for God's mission in our worship ministries—the resources, the people, the artistic giftedness? How many lives will be impacted by the gospel if we invest those resources in strategic community missions?

In *Missions: Biblical Foundations and Contemporary Strategies*, Gailyn Van Rheenen wrote, "In a real sense, mission is the very lifeblood of the church. As the body cannot survive without blood, so the church cannot survive without mission. Without blood the body dies; without mission the church dies. As the physical body becomes anemic without sufficient oxygen-carrying red blood cells, so the church becomes anemic if it does not express its faith. Mission is the force that gives the body of Christ vibrancy, purpose, and direction. When the church neglects its role as God's agent for mission, it is actually neglecting its own lifeblood."[3] Wow, what a statement! Is the evangelical church today actually bleeding away its lifeblood by trying to horde our giftedness inside the church building? Statistics show we are in dire need of a transfusion because we have put all our hope in attractional strategies inside the churches.

> Don't you have a saying, 'It's still four months until harvest'? I tell you, open your eyes and look at the fields! They are ripe for harvest. John 4: 35, NIV

3. Van Rheenen, *Missions: Biblical Foundations and Contemporary Strategies*, 31.

Can you see the harvest? Lives without Christ are fertile ground for seeds of the gospel. But like a farmer, our vision and motivation go beyond the planting. Can you envision the coming harvest before the field has even begun to sprout, while the seeds are deep in the ground? Joining God to harvest our world takes faith to see the unseen, then hard work to cultivate the crop. In God's harvest, he is the farmer directing the process, and we are his field hands. Joining his mission means we must roll up our sleeves and get our hands in the earth.

In the first church I served, we spent major amounts of time and effort joining forces with other local churches to present large productions. Our intent was to attract non-believers in our town to experience the gospel. In my next church, I started a community chorus for that same purpose. These were valuable worship experiences and enriched the spiritual and artistic lives of the participants. But they did little to move us out of the church and into our community. From there I went to a church that produced a large living Christmas tree presentation annually. In my last stop in local church ministry, I produced and directed a Christmas pageant aimed at evangelizing our community and region. Twenty-eight years of ministry were invested in those four churches with many long hours spent on productions.

For decades, music ministries have put tremendous effort into living Christmas trees, passion plays, patriotic programs, and other multimedia extravaganzas. As worship experiences, these productions can be valuable to express our love for God, proclaim the gospel, and inspire us to be disciples on mission. But they must not be our only strategy for outreach. Our primary strategy must be to mobilize Christians, sending them into their circles of influence with the gospel. I'm not saying that celebrative worship events have no place in a church's outreach strategy. I am saying that they must not be our only strategy or even our primary strategy. If we really want to give a gift to our community, we must go where they are, ask them what they need, then proceed to meet those needs. Then when we present a worship celebration, we can include stories of lives changed through our missions work.

This missional intent was fulfilled in the last of the four churches I served. In that church my ministry became refocused on mission to my community. Three mission opportunities had great impact on my life and ministry there. First, our youth minister and I partnered to take our youth group on mission to our town and region. Budget cuts forced us to develop local mission projects after the 9/11 attack on the World Trade Center.

First, we would target a community. Each day there, our youth minister coordinated home renovation crews and I coordinated mission Vacation Bible Schools in a park, apartment complex, or mobile home community. Each evening we teamed up to lead our youth music groups to do outreach concerts in the target community. The relationships built during a week of intensive service in one location were transformational, both for our participants and those we were serving. We presented these mission projects several times annually in our own community and local resort areas. Eventually this mission-music partnership grew to regularly involve 50 to 100 youth in home renovations, sport camps, beach ministry, mission Vacation Bible School, and mission block parties. I was hooked. The growing maturity we saw in our youth was reflected in both their commitment to discipleship and their depth of worship. Their lives were going full circle.

Second, I became active in the fledgling arts council of our town, serving as president for two years. Third, during my last five years, I served as musical director for an award-winning community theatre in the adjacent city, giving six weeks or so annually to recruit, audition, train and direct their annual Broadway musical show cast. The relationships developed in the arts council and community theatre gave me a wonderful context for personal mission.

I cannot adequately express the fulfillment these mission experiences brought to my life and ministry. Just as we had seen in our youth group, mission involvement ignited my commitment to deeper personal discipleship and worship. Going full circle, the cycle of worship-discipleship-mission dawned in my own life. The ministry opportunities through my community involvement outside the church were abundant. I was able to build friendships and working relationships with countless friends in all stages of spiritual need and spiritual development. I was able to point many friends to the power and grace of Jesus Christ. My vision for the harvest was enlarged. Yet, I could have done even more had I been more intentional in those opportunities.

It is a difficult journey of learning and faith to let God transform our thinking into the missional mindset. But there is joy and excitement when God shows you a new life more closely aligned with his Word. And joy is multiplied when you are able to bring along others to join you in the fields of harvest. In 2008, God called me to serve the South Carolina Baptist Convention as worship and music director. After two years in this position, I felt God calling me to start a movement of church musicians and worship leaders to become worshipers on mission. The vision God gave was to revitalize our worship ministries by becoming missionaries in our communities. In South Carolina, we are calling this movement M3: The MusicArts Mission Movement. Along the journey, I have learned that a movement is far more than starting another church program. A movement has motion only when we are following God and he is moving people to join him on mission. God is always on the move.

> Jesus said, "As the Father has sent me, I am sending you."
> John 20:21, NIV

What is the methodology of the missional mindset? I call it the Five-fingered-approach-to-handing-someone-the-gospel. It takes all five of these missional elements to hand someone the gospel on mission. Here is my five-fingered definition of missions that will help you hand the gospel to those around you:

- First finger: Meeting people at their point of need . . .
- Second finger: In your community . . .
- Third finger: On a regular basis . . .
- Fourth finger: To develop relationships . . .
- Thumbs up: Which lead to witnessing opportunities.

Church members typically think of missions as something we do away from our hometown. But joining God on his mission of redeeming the world starts with those around us. America is a huge mission field, and God is calling every Christian to be a missionary. If any element of the above definition is missing, we will fail to hand the gospel to those around us. If we assume we know their needs, we will miss them. If we only go once or twice a year, we will miss them. If we simply sing songs or hand out tracts without relationship, we will miss them. And if we do the first four without witnessing to the transformational power of Jesus, our efforts are no more than social gospel, and we miss the opportunity to offer them Christ.

The five-fingered-approach clearly defines what is missional and what is not missional. Simply presenting a church program on the street corner is not missional. Church programs designed for worship sound like a foreign language to those in our community. Granted, this is an easy way to check missions off our list and feel good about ourselves. However, this approach is largely ineffective for at least two reasons:

1. The right to share something as serious and confronting as the gospel must be earned. We earn the right to share the gospel by first meeting needs.
2. The gospel is best expressed in the context of relationship. Relationship is the context for transformational discipleship throughout Jesus' ministry. Effective mission happens in relationship.

We can't just throw an occasional bucket of water on the field and call ourselves farmers. But that's what we do when we present programs in our community once or twice a year and call it missions. We know it takes more to earn a listening ear, but we hesitate to invest in relationship and service.

Reggie McNeal has often reminded us in his writing and speaking that, for Christians, life is a mission trip. In his book, *Missional Communities,* McNeal wrote: "Through the years the program church redefined the game to match its scorecard and was not willing to be accountable for its impact in the world . . . The result was that what it means to act as salt and light was changed into church members' being marketing agents for church membership . . . Abundant life was contorted into church engagement. In the meanwhile, families are estranged, people go hungry, cynicism and fatalism hold hope hostage, while church leaders fret over meeting budgets and lament dwindling member support for an overstuffed church calendar."[4]

We must do better. There must be more.

Here are a few ideas to incorporate the five-fingered-approach-to-handing-someone-the-gospel in your community with your worship ministry:

- Adopt a community theater. Enlist worship ministry members as volunteer ushers for shows. Provide food for cast and crew for rehearsal evenings when they come straight to the theater from work.
- Adopt a museum. Worship ministry members sign up to serve as volunteers for children's programs, family days, or story-telling festivals at local art, history, or natural history museums.
- Adopt a public school music program. Assist your local public school music teachers by providing volunteers, sound equipment, spotlights, risers, or other needs.
- Present concerts in public venues on a weekly basis each summer. Feature your worship groups and individual artists. Train your church

4. McNeal, *Missional Communities: The Rise of the Post-Congregational Church*, 22–23.

members to begin casual conversations that can lead to relational witnessing among the audience. Face painters and balloon artists can also provide a witness to Christ.

- Plan a mission trip to your own community for your music and arts groups of all ages. Spend mornings and afternoons in construction work, music camps, sports camps, or mission Vacation Bible School in a nearby apartment complex or mobile home park. Arrange concerts in the evening in the same locations where you have served in the mornings. Train your team in personal witnessing for every situation encountered there.

What does your worship ministry include: praise band, worship choir, praise teams, ensembles, senior adult choir, instrumental groups, children's choir, handballs, soloists? Every one of them can be assigned an ongoing mission opportunity in your community. Hopefully, the above list will start your creative thinking. A more comprehensive list of potential music-arts mission projects is presented in chapter 15 of this book.

Let's start a music-arts mission movement that moves us where spirit and truth are at work, igniting worshiping disciples to be on mission. Let's move out to the places where God has been all along.

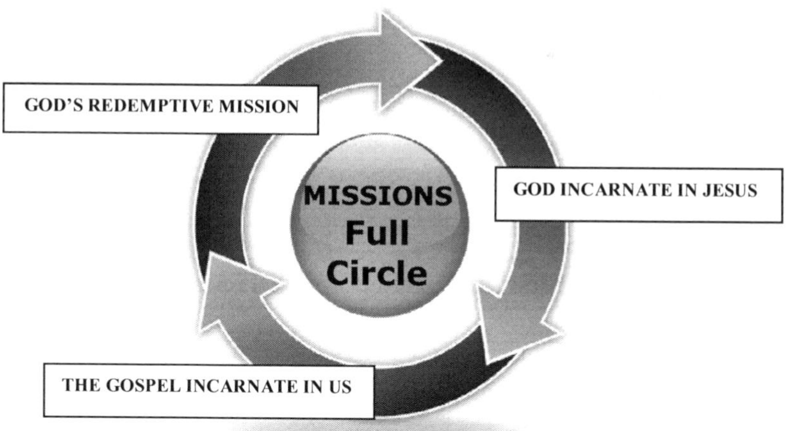

Diagram 4

Return to the Cross

O the deep, deep love of Jesus, vast unmeasured, boundless, free,
Rolling as a mighty ocean in its fullness over me.
Underneath me, all around me is the current of thy love,
Leading onward, leading homeward, to my glorious rest above.[5]

The two of us stood looking out over a crystal blue ocean on an international mission trip. Standing beside me was Tom Westmoreland, age 87, founding director of music for the South Carolina Baptist Convention. As we stood in awe of God's magnificent creation, Tom said, "You know, most people wear blinders. All they can see is their own little world. When I look at the ocean, I like to wonder where this water has been across the centuries. I wonder if I'm looking at water that flowed in the Jordan River when Jesus was baptized, or drawn from Jacob's well when Jesus encountered the Samaritan woman, or swirled around Paul when shipwrecked on his missionary journey. We never know where this water has been and who it has touched."

O the deep, deep love of Jesus, love of every love the best,
'Tis an ocean vast of blessing, 'tis a haven sweet of rest.
O the deep, deep love of Jesus, 'tis a heaven of heavens to me,
And it lifts me up to glory, for it lifts me up to thee.

The water of life pours from the cross of Christ to the world. Drink deeply of this water and quench your eternal thirst. Then go and share God's living water with our thirsty and dying world. Where will the water flow next?

Questions for Thought and Discussion

Have you seen a church sign recently that touts an attractional method? How did it read? How does its message fall short of Jesus' Great Commission?

Define attractional worship in your own words. Define missional worship in your own words. What are the differences in the results of these two philosophies of worship?

5. Francis, "O the Deep, Deep Love of Jesus," Public Domain.

Where is your church on the spectrum between attractional worship and attractive missional worship? How can worship in your church go full circle and grow worshiping disciples on mission?

How have you and others attempted to be missional but failed to complete the process and follow-through of the five-fingered-approach?

How can the five-fingered-approach-to-handing-someone-the-gospel enable you to join God's mission to redeem the world? List here the days of the week for the next ten days; then list beside each day of the week how you personally can put this methodology into practice each day and beyond.

How can your worship team put in action the five-fingered-approach on mission in your community?

10

God's Great Strategy: Four Missional Mandates

ALLOW ME TO INTRODUCE you to a modern-day Paul. This man is a missional artisan who surrenders his artistic giftedness to God. He models the five-fingered-approach-to-sharing-the-gospel.

Kerry Jackson was born and raised in Jackson, Miss. He accepted Jesus as Savior at age 9. Early in life he discovered his passion and giftedness for art. His pursuit for more knowledge and skill led him to obtain a bachelor of arts degree in painting from Mississippi State University. After several years working in the commercial art industry, he opened his own art studio. After six successful years, Jackson felt called by God to enter Christian ministry. Jackson sold his business and moved his family to Texas to attend seminary. Shortly after enrolling in seminary, Jackson discovered that God wanted to use the artist in him for his glory.

"While sitting in my car listening to music, waiting to pick up my daughter from piano lessons, God gave me a vision," Jackson recounted.[1]

"I literally saw a stage covered with painted scenes of the life of Christ utilizing special effects such as lighting, drama, etc. God even gave me the name, 'Drawing to the Rock,' at that time. The vision was so strong and clear that I wept and began praising and thanking God right there in my car."

After earning a master's degree in communication arts in 1993, Jackson accepted the position of exhibit designer with the North American Mission Board in Atlanta, Ga. From 2008 to 2010, he served as National Missionary to Cultural Creatives, coordinating efforts to reach this artistic people group in America. Meanwhile, Jackson continued captivating audiences across the country through "Drawing to the Rock" ministries.

1. Weeks, "Artist's handiwork draws others to Christ," Baptist Press, Feb. 17, 2003, wwwbaptistpress.com/bpnews.asp?id=15251.

Throughout his presentation he paints vignettes depicting mankind's sinful fall in the Garden of Eden culminating with Christ's victorious resurrection. While Jackson is creating his works of art onstage he is accompanied by recordings of biblical narratives and music by Christian artists.

In 2006, he and his wife, Twyla, began a home discipleship group for local artists. The Jacksons connected with the Atlanta arts community by volunteering at the High Museum of Art and hosting shows by guest artists at Jackson's studio near the museum. Their home group soon became a church known as Bezalel Church meeting in a downtown theater. In Exodus 31:1–6 we find the account of Bezalel. Bezalel was appointed by God to oversee a team of artisans charged with building and decorating the tabernacle. Jackson relishes the thought that the first person named in the Bible as being filled with the Spirit of God was an artist.

"If you have compassion, a gift, a talent, you can be on mission for God," according to Jackson.

God gives his followers four mandates in Scripture that compel us to be on mission for him. These are so prominent they are referred to as the great mandates. It's amazing, though, that most Christians have only heard of a few of these mandates. So we fail to understand that these mandates present God's strategy for bringing the world into relationship with him.

A mandate is an official command or instruction from an authority. If we truly recognize God as our authority, we must follow his mandates. Let's look at them and discover God's strategy to reach our communities.

> God blessed them, and God said to them, "Be fruitful, multiply, fill the earth, and subdue it." Genesis 1:28, HCSB

The first of God's four missional mandates is known as the "great cultural mandate." Here mankind is charged to subdue the earth and have dominion over it. God created all human beings with the innate nature to organize the earth regardless of whether they are in relationship with him or not. So the ways in which people subdue and have dominion over their lives lead to many different ways of organizing the world. This is called culture. Because the whole world is being constantly organized and reorganized by people, everything in this world is enculturated. We live our lives in the context of culture by God's design.

Cultural context determines style, language, dress, eating habits, social norms, etc. As people fulfill this mandate, they do so in harmony with their own geographic locale, climate, and resources. As we travel the earth, we see those near the ocean live differently from those in mountainous regions. We see people in tropical climates with cultural patterns contrasting those in frigid zones. But cultural variety also extends to local regions. For instance, people in the upstate of South Carolina are different from those in the midlands or low country. Differences abound in the way they relate to life, jobs, friends, church, etc., despite living within 100 miles or so of each other. And within each of those regions are other cultural groupings identified by ethnicity, education, income level, etc.

The cultural mandate helps us understand that God is the author of creative variety, that he created us to express diversity. God's gift of relationship in Christ is offered to all people of all cultures. Christians must realize that culture is a tool from God through which we communicate his gift of relationship. In Christ we find unity with God, but our cultural expressions of that unity are not uniform. God created it that way. He affirms our cultural diversity in the cultural mandate.

> The Lord said to Abram: Go out from your land, your relatives, and your father's house to the land that I will show you. I will make you into a great nation, I will bless you, I will make your name great, and you will be a blessing. I will bless those who bless you, I will curse those who treat you with contempt, and all the peoples on earth will be blessed through you. So Abram went, as the Lord had told him.
> Genesis 12:1–4b, HCSB

The second missional mandate from God is known as the "great covenant." God established this covenant with his chosen servant Abram, soon to be renamed Abraham, meaning "father of a great multitude." Abraham was a man whose faith in God empowered his life of obedience. Through him, God established the blood line from which Jesus came. God moved Abraham out of his comfort zone to forge a strong faith in him. God calls us, too, to move out of the comfort zone of church-ianity. Through Abraham's lineage of faith, God blessed the world with Jesus. Through our faith, God wants to bless our world.

God stands ready to make us a blessing to the world if we follow him in faith. The process of faith-building is not easy to endure. Like a weightlifting program, God will push us as far as we can go so our faith will endure a life of discipleship and mission. A lifestyle of worship-discipleship-mission builds faithful dependence on God in every situation. That's the level of faith that will empower us to maximum impact on mission. And, like Abraham, it begins by moving us out of our comfort zone.

> Love the Lord your God with all your heart, with all your mind, with all your soul. And love your neighbor as yourself.
> Matthew 22:39

God's third missional mandate to us is commonly known as the "great commandment." Here Jesus gave us his discipleship methodology in a nutshell. We are to set our highest priority on knowing and loving God. God wants us to love him with every fiber of our being. But this mandate is a two-part command. The second half of the mandate tells us to love others as much as we love ourselves. Loving others is a tall order for all of us, especially to love them as much as we love ourselves. But that's how Jesus tells us to live.

Why is showing love for God and others of such importance as we go on mission? Because the world can easily detect whether we are real or faking it. If we don't have God at the center of our lives and reflect his love in our relationships, they will see right through it. Nothing will discount our witness to the world quicker than trying to fake love for God or for people. We will be challenged at every turn as we work with people. Godly love must be the overriding characteristic of all we are and do.

> Then Jesus came to them and said, "All authority in heaven and on earth has been given to me. Therefore go and make disciples of all nations, baptizing them in the name of the Father and of the Son and of the Holy Spirit, and teaching them to obey everything I have commanded you. And surely I am with you always, to the very end of the age."
> Matthew 28:18–20, NIV

The fourth missional mandate is the Great Commission. We have looked at the Great Commission from several perspectives in previous chapters. When you get right down to it, this mandate simply means what it says. Here Jesus commanded us to go and make disciples. It cannot be much clearer. Jesus had gathered his earthly followers to speak to them for the last time before he ascended to heaven. We know that someone who is speaking for the last time is going to convey truths of utmost significance. Jesus' last words on earth pronounce five eternally significant truths he wants to make sure we know:

1. Since a mandate is a command given by an authority, Jesus wants us to know that he is the ultimate authority in the universe. His authority is given by his father God who created this universe. Jesus is the King of kings, Lord of lords, the authority of all authorities. He has demonstrated his pre-eminence in his virgin birth, perfect life, death, resurrection, and ascension.
2. Jesus wants us to know that he expects his disciples to join God's mission to redeem the world. With his last words on earth, Jesus was not suggesting, not asking, not pleading, but commanding every follower to make disciples of every people group on earth. *Ethnos,* the Greek word used here, is not correctly translated by the word "nations," as commonly quoted from the King James Version of the Bible. It actually translates "people groups." Traditional missionary organizations have defined people groups as ethno-linguistic groups. Curt Watke, Intercultural Institute for Contextual Ministry, reminds us that these groups can be more fluid, consisting of those who perceive themselves to be members of the same social category— nationality, race, ethnicity, social class, occupation, gender, religion, affinity, lifestyle, etc. Their identification with the group provides them emotional and value significance.[2]
3. Jesus wants us to know that we must go to the world. According to the Great Commission, it is not his plan to win the world by getting people into churches. We will win the world by getting the church into the world. The redemptive mission of God previously delivered through the chosen people of Israel is now being handed to every believer regardless of culture.
4. Jesus wants us to know that we should baptize those who follow him. Why would Jesus command us to do something as theologically controversial as baptizing disciples? Because baptism is the way we proclaim to the world that we are Jesus' disciple. Baptism dramatically portrays the death and burial of self and the resurrection to new life in Christ. Jesus clearly does not want his disciples to follow him in secret. Baptism is a public act of discipleship that symbolizes all it means to follow Christ. And he commands us to make it a priority.

2. Watke, "Understanding Your Missional Culturescape: a white paper on defining "people groups" for mission and ministry," www.missionalcyclopedia.org.

5. Jesus wants us to know that he expects us to teach disciples to obey his commands. There can be no discipleship without obedience to Christ's Biblical commands.

We are joining God in his great strategy for missions by following his mandates when we:

1. Embrace culture diversity as a tool to express the gospel;
2. Exercise total faith in God by leaving our comfort zone to follow him on mission;
3. Love him above all and love others as ourselves;
4. Go to all people groups to make disciples who follow Jesus in obedience.

> Again Jesus said, "Peace be with you!
> As the Father has sent me, I am sending you."
> John 20:21–22, NIV

In the previous chapter, I presented my five-fingered-approach-to-handing-someone-the-gospel. As I said there, it takes all five fingers to hand someone the gospel as we lead our worship ministries on mission to our community. Each element of this five-fingered strategy closely corresponds to God's missional mandates we have talked about above.

1. First finger. Meeting people at their point of need: The great commandment helps us know that God placed in each of us a deep need to love Him. That is humankind's greatest need. It tells Christians that we must love others enough to share how Christ meets that need. So often, we are held hostage by personal fear of being on mission to those around us. Loving others more than self is the key to overcoming that fear. The Great Commission commands us to go to them and not wait for them to come to us.
2. Second finger. In your community: The Great Commission calls us to go first to those locally before we move out to other lands. The great covenant calls us out of our comfort zones to move out in faith. The cultural mandate helps us understand that we must present the gospel in cultural languages that fit the people groups around us.
3. Third finger. On a regular basis: The great commandment tells us how to love others sacrificially with *agape* love. The great covenant calls us to go and live among them, believing in faith we will find God at work there.

4. Fourth finger. To develop relationships: The Great Commission compels us to teach the world about obedience. Jesus showed us that obedience is best taught in relationship. The great commandment tells us to embrace grace-filled relationships.
5. Thumbs up. Which lead to witnessing opportunities: This is the ultimate goal of all four of the great mandates. The Great Commission is a command to make disciples of all people groups. The great commandment shows God's intent that all people everywhere would first love him and then love others as themselves. The great covenant is a picture of dependence on God moving us out to the world to bring Christ to all people. The cultural mandate shows us how God gave us culture as the context through which we express his love for all.

And did you realize this? God's great strategy also reflects the circle of missional living, worship-discipleship-mission. Worship is "loving the Lord our God with all our heart and mind and soul," demonstrated both personally and as his church. Discipleship is following in faith, like Abraham, beyond our comfort zones with dependence on God. Missions is going to all people, loving them, baptizing and teaching obedience until they too go full circle in Christ.

When a worship ministry provides a weekly children's music group in a nearby apartment complex, they are following God's great strategy. As a worship ministry adopts local art studios and provides artists with coffee and donuts and volunteer time to develop witnessing relationships, they are following the great strategy. When we adopt a local community theater and provide meals for late night rehearsals, and supply volunteers to paint sets, make costumes, and usher, we are following the great strategy. As we love, serve, and connect with people to witness for Christ, we also grow personally in worship-discipleship-mission.

Recently an atheist sued a Texas county for placing a nativity scene on the courthouse lawn. But when diagnosed with a detached retina, he decided to drop the suit and focus on his health. A member of Sand Springs Church heard about the man's illness. She phoned her pastor and asked if he would pray about the church offering to help the man. The pastor said he needed no time to pray about it because Christ had already instructed the church to help those in need. So they did. And God worked through their efforts. Now the man who threatened the suit has had a shift in perspective and plans to move down the street from the church. He received enough money from the church to catch up on rent, bills, and taxes, plus they provided transportation to his eye doctor.

"We are literally still in a state of shock," the man said. "I feel like we are in the Twilight Zone."[3] This church has gone full circle in missional living.

> But in whatever anyone dares to boast—I am talking foolishly—I also dare: Are they Hebrews? So am I. Are they Israelites? So am I. Are they the seed of Abraham? So am I. Are they servants of Christ? I'm talking like a madman—I'm a better one: with far more labors, many more imprisonments, far worse beatings, near death many times. Five times I received 39 lashes from Jews. Three times I was beaten with rods by the Romans. Once I was stoned by my enemies. Three times I was shipwrecked. I have spent a night and a day in the open sea. If boasting is necessary, I will boast about my weaknesses. The God and Father of the Lord Jesus, who is praised forever, knows I am not lying. 2 Corinthians 11:21–25, 30–31, HCSB

Paul modeled God's great strategy with his life. In him we see a man sold out to God's mission to redeem the world. In the above Scripture, Paul's integrity was apparently under attack from one of his many detractors. So, against his own better judgment, ("I am talking foolishly . . . like a madman.") Paul chronicled the hardship that validated his status as a missionary for Christ. Time and again, he endured terrible circumstances and personal attack, yet he stayed the course as a worshiping disciple on mission. Let's look at the ways Paul reflected the great strategy.

1. The great cultural mandate: Paul, Hebrew from birth and citizen of Rome who spoke several languages, was uniquely gifted by God to "become all things to all people" (1 Cor. 9:22, NIV) on mission. He adapted to the community and people wherever he traveled, using the culture of that locale as common ground to build witnessing relationships. Paul understood that culture is a tool from God to connect people with him. Learning and communicating in the heart languages of those around him became second nature.
2. The great covenant: Paul, the ultimate Pharisee, shifted allegiance to Christ and traveled the world on his behalf. Paul modeled God's

3. Colter, "Atheist shocked when church helps with bills," *Southern Baptist Texan* newsletter, 2012, 8. www.brnow.org/News/April-2012?page=8.

covenant of faith: the grace of God manifested first in the Hebrew nation, ultimately was revealed in Jesus, then flowed to the whole world through his disciples. Acts 13 (HCSB) showed Paul in the synagogue in Antioch of Pisidia, preaching the gospel of Christ to his fellow Jews. He punctuated his testimony with phrases that demonstrate the Great Covenant: "Fellow Israelites and you Gentiles who worship God, listen to me!" (Acts 13:13); "Fellow children of Abraham, and you God-fearing Gentiles, it is to us that this message of salvation has been sent," (Acts 13:26); and "We tell you the good news: What God promised our ancestors he has fulfilled for us, their children, by raising up Jesus" (Acts 13:32). As Christ's missionary, Paul understood that God's mission is revealed in the whole history of mankind, not just in what God is doing for him right now.

3. The great commandment: Paul, the persecutor of Christians, was changed into a man of compassion when he encountered Christ. Paul preached the pure gospel in all its ramifications without regard to political correctness. Yet there was no doubt in his writings or in the way people responded to him that he was a man of great compassion and caring. "I, therefore, the prisoner in the Lord, urge you to walk worthy of the calling you have received, with all humility and gentleness, with patience, accepting one another in love, diligently keeping the unity of the Spirit with the peace that binds [us]" (Eph. 4:1, HCSB). As Christ's missionary, Paul cared for and loved people with the love of Jesus. His was not a soft love aimed at offending no one and being tolerant of all. Paul's love was tough and enduring. The Greek word *agape* means "sacrificial love," and it is the word Paul used throughout 1 Corinthians 13 as he defined love. Paul demonstrated that a worshiping disciple on mission reflects God's unconditional, sacrificial love to the world.

4. The Great Commission: Paul, champion of the Hebrew faith, was transformed into a disciple of Jesus and went on mission for him. In chapter six, I cited Paul's writings that demonstrate his heart for worship. Worship continually empowered Paul to join God on mission to redeem the world. In Acts 16:25-26 (HCSB), we see Paul and Silas worshiping in prison: "About midnight, Paul and Silas were praying and singing hymns to God, and the other prisoners were listening to them. Suddenly there was such a violent earthquake that the foundations of the prison were shaken. At once all the prison

doors flew open, and everyone's chains came loose." The story continues in verses 29–34: "The jailer called for lights, rushed in and fell trembling before Paul and Silas. He then brought them out and asked, 'Sirs, what must I do to be saved?' They replied, 'Believe in the Lord Jesus, and you will be saved—you and your household.' Then they spoke the word of the Lord to him and to all the others in his house. At that hour of the night the jailer took them and washed their wounds; then immediately he and his household were baptized. The jailer brought them into his house and set a meal before them; he was filled with joy because he had come to believe in God—he and his whole household."

The power of Paul's personal worship ignited his calling as a disciple on mission. His life fulfilled Christ's Great Commission mandate.

> Because we loved you so much, we were delighted to share with you not only the gospel of God but our lives as well. For you recall, brethren, our labor and hardship, how working night and day so as not to be a burden to any of you, we proclaimed to you the gospel of God. 1 Thessalonians 2:8–9, NIV

Like me, you may have assumed that Paul started churches according to an institutional church model. An institutional model for church planting would require finding a building in which to meet, securing furnishings, hiring staff, and promoting the first worship service to attract the community to the grand opening. But a study of Scripture shows that Paul's approach was not institutional. Instead, Paul used his giftedness as an artisan to serve his community and build relationships that led to sharing the gospel. His missional heart led him to present the gospel of Christ in every cultural context, in the marketplace to Gentiles and in the synagogue to Jews. Paul embodied the concept of being on mission rather than the attractional model we so easily promote today.

Paul reminded the Christians at Thessalonica that he went beyond simply being a figurehead and shared daily life with them. Paul truly modeled the five-finger-approach-to-handing-someone-the-gospel. He met them at their point of need in his community on a regular basis to build relationships that led to witnessing opportunities.

While Paul was not a worship leader or musician, he was in fact an artisan. An artisan is defined by www.dictionary.com as "a person skilled in an applied art; a craftsperson who makes a high-quality, distinctive product in small quantities, usually by hand and using traditional methods."[4] An artisan enriches daily life by producing useful and artistically pleasing artifacts. What was Paul's artistic gift that he used as a vocation to serve his community? He was a leatherworking artisan, making and repairing tents and other items to support himself (Acts 18:3).

But Paul's tent-making was more than a job. His craft was his doorway into the community and into relationship with his target group, like Jackson in the example above. From this vocation arose daily opportunities to share with customers and other merchants. Those relationships led to invitations to speak to gatherings in homes, in the market, or at the town square. Through Paul's witness, some came to believe and trust in Jesus as Savior and Lord. Groups of believers began to gather in homes to worship, grow in discipleship, and move out on mission. These home groups became mission outposts which grew into churches. And there you have it: the most basic element of effective church planting—worshiping disciples on mission starting home groups to grow into house churches.

> For we are not proclaiming ourselves but Jesus Christ as
> Lord, and ourselves as your slaves because of Jesus.
> 2 Corinthians 4:5, HCSB

Here is another modern-day Paul. This individual is also a missional artisan following God's great strategy and modeling the five-fingered-approach-to-sharing-the-gospel.

Steve Fairchild fulfills his mission to artists in a completely different setting than the Jacksons. Fairchild went to live with his grandparents after his parent's divorce. His grandparents took him to church every Sunday and on Wednesday nights. There he learned the basic facts of the gospel but church left him confused and frustrated. The pastor preached against smoking but lit up a cigarette anytime he worked on his car. Church members smiled and hugged at church but talked hatefully about each other all week. Fairchild said, "As a child, I remember being told that dancing and going to movies was sinful. Then the rules changed and movies and dancing were okay. I used to wonder what happened to all the people that went to movies and died before they changed the rules. As I grew up I wanted no part of church or organized religion."

Fairchild's mother eventually remarried and brought him home. As professional musicians, his mother and stepfather traveled with several

4. www.dictionary.com.

prominent country music artists. So when Fairchild could break away, he took to the road as a country musician himself.

He remembered, "When I began my career in show business, Jesus was the last thing I was thinking about. I was in the fast lane making lots of money as a Garth Brooks tribute artist, having lots of fun, and touring all over the world. I thought if I was just a good person, I would be okay."

But his thinking changed when he met his wife. She shared how important Jesus was in her life and that she would never marry someone who was not a believer in Christ.

"I can sacrifice an hour in church if I get to marry the most beautiful girl I've ever met," he thought. "So that's what I did while we were dating and in the first two years of marriage. I went to church for her, not me."

One Sunday morning the pastor asked, "What is keeping you from a relationship with Jesus?"

It was a searing question, but Fairchild had plenty of answers.

The pastor continued, "Some of you are carrying around excuses like bricks in a backpack. Let them go and come to Jesus."

Suddenly, like Paul on the Damascus road, it was as if Fairchild was the only person in the room. He heard Jesus' voice, "Steve, what is your excuse?"

Steve replied with his standard answer, "There are too many hypocrites in church."

He heard Jesus ask again, "What does that have to do with your relationship with me?"

"I don't like how they change the rules!" Fairchild countered.

But through his every excuse, Jesus' question was the same.

Fairchild said, "My life changed that day. I gave my whole life to Jesus. My backpack of excuses fell to the ground, and I was free for the first time in my life."

Then reality set in. The next day, Fairchild went to the theater where for many years he had been performing 12 shows a week impersonating Garth Brooks. There was sin all around him in the language, attitudes, and actions of his fellow artists.

He said, "The biggest shock was not all the mess that was happening around me, but how I had lived in that mess without ever seeing it before."

The next morning he met with his pastor. He shared that he was going to have to quit his job to avoid the evil around him.

The pastor looked him in the eye and said, "How will anyone come out of that darkness if you are not there to show them the light?"

A missionary was born.

Fairchild completes his story by saying, "Since 2000, I have traveled the world spreading the good news of Jesus Christ disguised as Garth Brooks. Meanwhile, I became an elder in our church and served as worship leader. In 2010 our pastor became ill and died unexpectedly. The following October, I was chosen to succeed him as pastor of our church, Low Country Community Church in Myrtle Beach, S.C. Many of the artists I have worked with across the years, now come to my church. I don't preach in my cowboy hat but I do still perform as Garth. Every time I sing 'Friends in Low Places,' I am reminded of people in low places looking desperately for life's answer. Christ is the answer. We have been commissioned to go and make disciples for him. If God can use a Garth Brooks impersonator, he can use anybody!"[5]

Return to the Cross

On a hill faraway stood an old rugged cross,
the emblem of suffering and shame;
And I love that old cross where the dearest and best for a world
of lost sinners was slain.
So I'll cherish the old rugged cross,
till my glories at last I lay down.
I will cling to the old rugged cross,
and exchange it someday for a crown.[6]

The perfect Savior of the world died on a criminal's cross. At the foot of the cross, watching her son's blood and breath drain away, stood Jesus' mother. Grieving alongside her were her best friends. We don't know how many of Jesus' 12 disciples stayed throughout that horrible day of agony. At least one disciple remained, the one whom Jesus loved, probably John, the writer of this account in John 19. When Jesus saw his mother there, and the disciple whom he loved standing nearby, he said to his mother, "Dear woman, here is your son," and to the disciple, "Here is your mother." From that time on, this disciple took her into his home.

5. Personal correspondence with author.
6. Bennard, "The Old Rugged Cross," Public Domain.

In the old rugged cross, stained with blood so divine,
such a wonderful beauty I see;
For 'twas on that old cross Jesus suffered and died
to pardon and sanctify me.
So I'll cherish the old rugged cross,
till my glories at last I lay down.
I will cling to the old rugged cross,
and exchange it someday for a crown.

The word of God made flesh takes our sin into his flesh to pay our debt. The all-powerful son of the eternal God became a caring son to his earthly mother. The one who calls all to be his disciples assigned a single disciple to care for a single person. So many amazing paradoxes converge at the cross of Christ. Is there room at the cross for one more? See Jesus looking from the cross into your eyes. Who in this world has he assigned to your care? Will you take them into your heart, your home, your heaven?

Questions for Thought and Discussion

Were any of God's four great mandates new to you? Summarize in your own words how the four mandates work together to form God's strategy for missions in your community.

What are some ways you can embrace God's great strategy in your own life by being on mission every day?

How will the five-fingered-approach-to-handing-someone-the-gospel better enable you to fulfill this great strategy?

How do you personally identify with Paul and his missional approach to daily life? How do you personally identify with Kerry Jackson and Steve Fairchild in their missional approach to daily life?

What would your life look like if you were to use your daily relationships as missional opportunities?

11

Culture: A Tool from God

And the Word became flesh and dwelt among us.
John 1:24, KJV

IN OUR LAST CHAPTER, we discovered the great cultural mandate from God. In this mandate, found in Genesis 1:8, God commanded us to subdue and have dominion over the earth. Culture grows out of the variety of ways in which mankind fulfills this command to organize the earth. Are you having questions about this concept and how culture impacts worship, discipleship, and mission? Don't feel alone. I had many questions about that same thing as God brought me through my pilgrimage from attractional thinking to a missional mindset across these past few years. Let's call a "time-out" and discuss culture.

When Jesus came into the world, he didn't come as just any man. God gave Jesus a cultural identity because everything in the world exists in the context of culture. Again, culture results from humankind's efforts to organize the earth as God commanded in the cultural mandate. So culture is not an evil thing. Culture is a "given" whenever we talk about life on earth. Jesus himself was not just a man but a Jewish man. He was not just a Jewish man, but a first-century-native-of-Palestine, born-in-Bethlehem, son-of-Joseph-and-Mary, living-in-Nazareth, working-as-a-carpenter, unmarried Jewish man. All of those elements of his identity on earth are cultural. Obviously, God does not despise culture or see it as an enemy of his mission because when Jesus became a man, he came into the full cultural context God had chosen for him.

How do we know that the cultural context of Jesus was no accident? We know this because Jesus' cultural characteristics fulfilled many ancient prophecies foretold across centuries by spokesmen of God. In other words, God had been preparing a specific cultural context for Jesus from before the foundation of the earth. God created culture and then used it as a tool to place his Son just where he wanted him!

Cultural context is a powerful force for all of us. This truth is well-illustrated in a funny story told to me by Larry Rice, retired missionary to Venezuela. Larry recounted how an American guest speaker came to the Venezuelan college where Larry was teaching. Since Larry was to be the translator for the guest American, the speaker told him that he planned to begin his address with a joke and shared it with him. Apologetically, Larry pointed out to the speaker that the college students would not understand the joke because the humor did not translate into Venezuelan culture. But the American speaker insisted that his joke was understandable by all and assured Larry that the students would find it funny. So the guest began his speech with Larry translating. Sure enough, when the speaker told the joke, the college students laughed loudly.

"See there," whispered the American triumphantly to Larry, "I told you the students would get my joke."

What the speaker did not know was that in his introduction of the speaker, Larry had told the students that the American was going to start by telling a joke. The guest, not understanding the Venezuelan language, was unaware as Larry told the students, "His joke will not make sense to you because it is from American culture. So when I tell you to laugh, just laugh real loud, and we will help this man feel at home."

As instructed, their fake laughter made the joke appear to be a great hit, though the students could not understand it in their cultural context.

Again, culture is a tool from God to be used to connect people with him. Culture is not a natural enemy of God. Of course, it can be used for evil or good, but it has no inherent quality of good or evil. Francis Shaeffer wrote: "Let me say firmly that there is no such thing as a godly style or an ungodly style. The more one tries to make such a distinction, the more confusing it becomes."[1]

Instead of declaring culture as our enemy, the church needs to understand that the gospel can embody cultural context as a means of identification and communication. Christ embodied this truth in his incarnation. He

1. Shaeffer, *Art and the Bible*, 76.

became a man in a specific cultural context so that we could identify with him. My favorite quote about Christ's incarnation is from Dorothy Sayers, writing in *Christian Letters to a Post Christian World*: "For whatever reason God chose to make man as he is—limited and suffering and subject to sorrows and death—he had the honesty and courage to take his own medicine. He can exact nothing from man that he has not exacted from himself. He has himself gone through the whole human experience, from the trivial irritations of family life and the cramping restrictions of hard work and lack of money to the worst horrors of pain and humiliation, defeat, despair, and death. He was born in poverty and died in disgrace and thought it well worthwhile."[2]

God in Christ took on the context of culture to communicate his love, and now he is calling his church to do the same.

Of course, the most obvious calling card of culture is style. "Indigenous," a term meaning "natural or inborn," is helpful in understanding the concept of native culture. Indigenous style most easily identifies who we are in the context of our own culture. But again, just as with culture, we sinful humans tend to condemn any style that is not our own. Whether musical style, architectural style, dress and fashion, or a myriad of other things, our sinful nature aspires to put our favorite style on the worship throne and condemn other styles. Dwayne Moore, in his Bible study on worship entitled *Pure Praise*, noted: "The Bible simply makes no reference to a preferred style . . . So, if God's Word is apparently not concerned with style, why should we be so up in arms about it?"[3]

When we deify our personal preferences, we stop using culture as a tool and put ourselves on the throne. Again, this is idolatry. Christians must join God as he uses culture and style to connect both Christians and non-Christians to himself.

While on a mission project to a Latin American country, we worked with a local pastor in our host country. Upon arrival, we asked him if our singing group could sing a gospel song for their worship service that was written in the salsa style. He graciously explained that he would prefer that we not sing songs in that style. He shared that he and his wife had accepted Christ in their adult years. In their younger pre-Christian years, the two of them frequented bars and dance halls where salsa style prevailed. For him, this style of music represented his former life before accepting Christ. So

2. Sayers, *Christian Letters to a Post Christian World*, page unknown.

3. Moore, *Pure Praise*, 110.

our group politely agreed to omit the salsa style praise song from our concert there. After spending a week working shoulder-to-shoulder for Christ in his town, the pastor came back to me before our final concert. He wanted me to know that he had changed his mind and wanted us to sing the salsa style praise song for our final concert. I asked him what brought him to this change of heart. He shared with me that his two college-age sons had pulled him aside and talked with him. They explained that salsa style did not have sinful connotations for them. The sons said that the exciting salsa rhythms actually captured for them and their generation the joy of loving and serving God. So the pastor relented. He said that it was time he stopped being the keeper of standards based on his prejudice from the past. He said he was ready to give God the salsa style to use for his glory.

While we are the gospel incarnate to a culture, the church must never stoop to embrace popular fads as a means of fitting comfortably into secular culture. Beth Moore, expressed this concept well in her study of Daniel: "They (Daniel and his friends) learned the language, literature, and customs all right, but only so God could use them in the midst of it. They read the language of their culture with the lens of God. Thereby, they became culturally relevant without becoming spiritually irrelevant."[4]

> Though I am free and belong to no man, I make myself a slave to everyone, to win as many as possible. To the Jews I became like a Jew, to win the Jews. To those under the law I became like one under the law (though I myself am not under the law), so as to win those under the law. To those not having the law I became like one not having the law (though I am not free from God's law but am under Christ's law), so as to win those not having the law. To the weak I became weak, to win the weak. I have become all things to all men so that by all possible means I might save some. I do all this for the sake of the gospel, that I may share in its blessings.
> 1 Corinthians 9:19–23, NIV

When a classically trained singer hears a pop singer's signature style featuring light resonance, breathiness, de-emphasized consonants, and overdone diphthongs they usually respond, "How strange and contrived that singer sounds." When a pop singer hears a classically trained singer's signature style featuring full support and resonance, over-enunciated consonants, and pure vowels with full vibrato they usually respond, "How

4. Moore, *Daniel: Lives of Integrity, Words of Prophecy*, 26.

strange and contrived that singer sounds." Of course, the same would be true for a country singer, an urban music artist, an oriental vocalist, or a jazz singer. Their reactions are based on their cultural context which informs and determines their personal taste. If Christian singers want to target a specific audience with the message of Christ, then they must learn the musical style that speaks to that audience. Like a Nashville studio artist who makes a living by learning to manipulate their voice to sing all styles, a missional artist must adapt. To do anything less is to be a culture snob. Culture snobs are not just limited to classical music. They are fans of any style who deify their favorite and demonize others—country, gospel, rap, jazz, pop, hip-hop, you name it.

The above Scripture indicates that God wants us to understand that culture is a tool to connect people with him in their real-life context. This scriptural principle also applies to other cultural signifiers such as personal fashion, hairstyle, jewelry, interior decorations, architecture, etc.

A Christian newsletter recently became a forum for a fiery month-long debate between fine Christian people over whether appropriate dress for church is a tie and jacket or jeans and a golf shirt. I have heard heated arguments over whether appropriate architecture for a Christian church is a large warehouse with portable seating and a stage, or a traditional church sanctuary with pews, choir loft, stained glass windows, and a pulpit. I have tried to explain lovingly to someone as mad as a hornet why the youth choir was not wearing neckties or dresses when they sang in resort areas. 1 Corinthians 9:22–23 tells us that appropriateness must be determined by the cultural context of those we are trying to reach. Of course, we are never to deem appropriate anything that is sinful or wrong by biblical standards or could be a stumbling block to others coming to faith in Christ.

My father-in-law is a classy businessman from the old school of suits and ties, and my bearded son is a nouveau hippy. Both of them love God and have served him faithfully in their contexts. It's fun to watch them poke fun at each other about what is appropriate in facial hair and fashion. After attending a large regional conference involving young church leaders, my father-in-law asked me what the conference was like. I told him that it was like worshiping with 15,000 young church leaders who look just like my son.

He exclaimed, "How could you stand to be with that many people who look like that and worship like that?"

I replied, "Because we were focused on worshiping God together."

"Oh, okay," he relented, "I hadn't thought about that."

Worship wars result when we decide that our own style is preferred by God. Worship wars result when we become the self-appointed keeper of standards and try to force our preference on others. Worship wars result when we forget that God created worship for himself and gave us the tool of culture to connect others with him.

J.D. Greear, pastor of Summit Church in Raleigh/Durham, N.C. recently wrote on his blog: "God created us to glorify Him in art, and when we do so we fulfill his purpose in creation. However, our desire to produce good art must be balanced with the fact that God has called us to leverage our resources for the spread of the Gospel. Thus, our (a local church's) desire to produce good art should be balanced with the urgency of the mission."[5]

It's time for us to repent of the sin that makes us culture snobs about our favorite language, style, dress, music, architecture, and anything else that we place on the throne of our worship in place of God himself.

> When the day of Pentecost came, they were all together in one place. Suddenly a sound like the blowing of a violent wind came from heaven and filled the whole house where they were sitting. They saw what seemed to be tongues of fire that separated and came to rest on each of them. All of them were filled with the Holy Spirit and began to speak in other tongues as the Spirit enabled them. Now there were staying in Jerusalem God-fearing Jews from every nation under heaven. When they heard this sound, a crowd came together in bewilderment, because each one heard them speaking in his own language. Utterly amazed, they asked: "Aren't all these men who are speaking Galileans? Then how is it that each of us hears them in his native language?"
> Acts 2:1–8, NIV

Christians must communicate in the cultural languages of the people group to whom they are sent. On the day of Pentecost, Peter preached the gospel in his Aramaic language. Yet people from all across the known world who were present that day heard Peter's message in their own native language. Miraculously, Peter's words were translated by the Holy Spirit into the language of the listeners. God was at work in Peter that day using language as a cultural tool to communicate the gospel of Christ.

5. Greear, www.jdgreear.com/my_weblog/2010/07.

Spoken language is the mode by which we express ourselves and communicate our thoughts verbally. Language is a set of symbols that signify certain realities and convey meaning. We combine the letters t, a, b, l, and e to signify a real object that we can place our dinner on. Similarly, art forms such as music, fashion, visual art, architecture, dance, etc., express life and communicate thought. So, artistic forms truly are cultural languages. Consequently, artistic style, while not inherently good or evil, certainly can convey cultural context and theological meaning. A cathedral communicates God's majesty and glory while the simple country church communicates God's accessibility. The "Hallelujah" Chorus from Handel's "Messiah" often brings the audience to their feet, while a quiet hymn may move us to prayer, then a praise chorus might cause us to clap along or lift our hands heavenward. These are all culturally programmed responses to an artistic style. After Sunday worship, a close friend told me, "I dread singing 'How Great Thou Art' because it was sung at my mother's funeral and it brings back the feeling of grief." For this lady, this great song of worship does not signify praise but sorrow.

As worship leaders, we must carefully discern our cultural context to understand what certain styles signify. Just as we need to communicate the gospel of Christ in the spoken and written language of the target group, so too must we communicate in their artistic and stylistic languages. The church you serve is not in the same cultural context as any other church. Every church in every community has a unique calling to a unique cultural context. Don't settle for duplicating a style that is working in another church simply because you assume it will work for your church, too. When we follow the leading of the Spirit of God, guided every step by his Word of Truth, we can forget about following a trend. Missional worship comes through much prayer, studying his Word, studying the community where he has placed us, and leading Christians to grow as disciples and become missionaries to their community. That's when our worship will come alive. Not because we have the latest technical equipment or a cool new format, but because we have a mission.

Are you working to be the best church "in" your community or to be the best church "for" your community? Baseball players and golfers are always hoping to hit the ball on the "sweet spot" to get the most "carry." Find the cultural "sweet spot" for your church's worship and then stay in it to "carry" them full circle.

On a mission tour to Taiwan, I worshiped in a Chinese-speaking church. Could I truly worship there? Yes, because I brought God my heart, mind, and soul and presented them to him. But I could not sing the songs in Mandarin or understand the pastor's sermon. I could pray during prayer times, but I could not understand their spoken prayers. So I worshiped God personally, but I could not be taught or convicted by God's Word because it was presented in another language. To stay in Taiwan and continue to go to this Chinese-speaking church, I would have to learn their language. Otherwise, the language barrier would have caused me to dry up as a disciple and forced me to find an English speaking church. Yet in our own churches, we often accuse those who fail to participate in unfamiliar styles as spiritually immature or narrow. For this reason, many call blended worship the "equal opportunity offender." The truth is that we must meet church members where they are because most people will remain primarily immersed in the particular culture where God has placed them.

This brings us to the issue of heart language. All of us have a cultural context in which God has placed us. But when life "rocks our world," we turn to our God-given heart language to express our deepest feelings. For instance, when you lose your job, how do you express your emotions? When a loved one dies, what music do you listen to, what phrases do you say, and what comfort foods do you eat? Those things that express your deepest feelings in moments of deepest emotion are your heart language. If we really want to connect people with God in worship, we must offer them that opportunity in their heart language. It stands to reason that to move people to a change of heart we should communicate the gospel in their heart language. We must learn the heart languages of the people to whom God is sending us.

Many times, leading a worship song and looking across the congregation, I have seen couples standing there looking at me in total bewilderment. They might be wearing jeans and T-shirts in the midst of folks in dresses, coats and ties and singing hymns. Or they might be wearing dresses, coats and ties in the midst of the flip-flop crowd who are rocking along with a praise band. It's obvious that they have come to church expecting one style of worship but find themselves in a totally different culture. Both are obviously caught in a worship language disconnect. Is the couple to blame? Are they being narrow and spiritually immature? No, they are demonstrating the innate characteristics of cultural context and heart language. Again, we cannot expect people to connect best with God in a cultural language that is not their own. God created cultural variety on purpose, so we need to celebrate it and use it to connect people with him.

I often hear ministerial staff fuss at their church members for not accepting other styles. I've probably been guilty of fussing like that myself. Unfortunately, this often occurs when the staff wants to force their favorite style on the congregation and the members are not open to that change. Will Christians ever grow in Christ to the point where they will be able to connect with God in a different heart language? In other words, can spiritual maturity override cultural context? The truth is that we will always connect to God best in our own heart language. It's how God wired us. Yet as we are transformed in Christ to think more sacrificially, we should become more open to other cultures and their unique styles. Across two or three generations, cultural openness will allow similar cultures to become unified as one.

Vital Contextual Worship is a term I use to avoid using the stylistic signifiers such as "contemporary" or "traditional" as our target. Vital Contextual Worship aims at worship that transcends style:

- Vital: alive, dynamic, and flowing with energy.
- Contextual: accurately reflects the cultural context of your community of believers to powerfully connect them with God and ignite them to discipleship and mission.
- Worship: focused primarily on God's "worth-ship" by glorifying him and calling us to live as his children 24/7.

Vital Contextual Worship gives me a term that encompasses the concepts discussed throughout this book. I hope you will find the term useful as a goal in your worship ministry.

> Some men came down from Judea and began to teach the brothers, "Unless you are circumcised according to the custom prescribed by Moses, you cannot be saved." But after Paul and Barnabas had engaged them in serious argument and debate, they arranged for Paul and Barnabas and some others of them to go up to the apostles and elders in Jerusalem concerning this controversy . . . Peter stood up and said . . . "Why, then, are you now testing God by putting on the disciples' necks a yoke that neither our forefathers nor we have been able to bear? On the contrary, we believe we are saved through the grace of the Lord Jesus, in the same way they are." Then the whole assembly fell silent and listened to

> Barnabas and Paul describing all the signs and wonders God had done through them among the Gentiles . . . Then the apostles and the elders, with the whole church, decided to select men from among them and to send them to Antioch with Paul and Barnabas . . . For it was the Holy Spirit's decision—and ours—to put no greater burden on you than these necessary things. Acts 15:1–2, 7, 9, 11–12, 22, 28, HCSB

Paul could have had "rock star status" by remaining in the church in Jerusalem after his conversion. But he chose to leave his comfort zone and go share Christ with the world. Back home in Jerusalem, trouble was brewing. There were those in the Jerusalem church who insisted that circumcision should be a requirement for acceptance of Christ. They would require this sign of faithfulness given to Abraham in ancient days not just for Jewish males but for all male converts of any ethnicity. Those who argued for circumcision were proponents of institutionalism, keepers of standards, who would force this external condition on those coming to Christ as Savior. Peter, James, and Simeon were leaders in the Jerusalem church. As original disciples of Jesus who had walked with him on earth, they knew the road to salvation could not be paved with institutional requirements. So their courageous response went against the grain of popular feeling in the church. Peter, James, and Simeon summoned Paul to Jerusalem, listened to the arguments from both sides, and ruled in favor of the unhindered circle of worship-discipleship-mission as the model for relationship with Christ.

A great setback to the spread of the gospel of Christ was averted that day. The mission of God to redeem the whole world, not just the Jewish people, continued to move forward. The three leaders of the church exercised their prophetic voice and re-commissioned Paul to go to the neighboring people groups as a worshiping disciple on mission. Meanwhile, the Jerusalem church was freed to do the same in their own community without the restriction of religious requirements. Things that once were helpful to the gospel can become a hindrance to the gospel when they become ours.

But God used the Jerusalem Council in another way, too, that day. Our all-knowing Father granted Paul and his partners on mission the rare opportunity to share their methodology with the home church. Paul was able to tell how God was using him as a tentmaker to infiltrate communities for Christ. No doubt, the stories Paul shared of his work as a missional artisan inspired and taught the Jerusalem church. The five-fingered-approach-to-handing-someone-the-gospel came alive in Paul's testimony. In stories like Paul's, we can catch a glimpse of all God is calling us to be as his missionary. In stories of missional obedience, we too hear the call, "Whom shall I send?" and can confidently respond, "Here am I, send me!"

The concept of culture as a God-given tool to connect people with him has not been taught well in our churches and Christian schools. There have even been times in the history of the Christian mission movement when missionaries themselves did not understand the concepts of cultural context and heart language. They tried to force their own culture on those to whom they were sent. Instead of adopting the native dress, language, diet, music, art, etc., they resolutely demanded that the native people accept western dress, the English language, American food, English hymns, and western architecture. Instead of being God incarnate to those they came to serve, they insisted that the native people incarnate the imported culture of the missionary. The obvious results of this kind of cultural snobbery are barriers to acceptance of Christ and failure to plant churches that are indigenous to native people. We must not force another culture to adopt our culture before they can accept Christ. Can you see how self-centered and egotistical this approach is? It is the height of idolizing my own culture to make my style and tastes a prerequisite for others to know and follow Christ.

But wait a minute. We do this all the time in our own churches. This cultural snobbery is a notorious characteristic of the institutional church. We see it in church-ianity where stylistic peripherals become significant priorities. We think that if new churches are started in our community they should certainly worship in the same style we do. It's easy for us to idolize our favorite style and demonize others. When will we realize that culture is not a tool with which to beat others over the head until they accept my way of doing things? Culture is a God-given tool to meet people where they are and connect them to him. But there is another lesson to be applied from this all-important truth. And this next lesson may truly revolutionize the way you think of your own church and the way you worship. Keep reading!

> Then they said, "Come, let us build ourselves a city, with a tower that reaches to the heavens, so that we may make a name for ourselves . . ." But the Lord came down to see the city and the tower that the men were building. The Lord said, "If as one people speaking the same language they have begun to do this, then nothing they plan to do will be impossible for them. Come, let us go down and confuse their language so they will not understand each other." So the Lord scattered them from there over all the earth . . .

> there the Lord confused the language of the whole world. From there the Lord scattered them over the face of the whole earth. Genesis 11:4–9, NIV

This biblical story is commonly referred to as the Tower of Babel. Here are men who decided to try to transcend God by building a monument to their own power and their own ingenuity. Do situations like that ever occur in churches today?

The young worship leader came to his new church assignment with excitement. But he encountered a congregation there that had worshiped basically the same way for the past 30 years. Most of the members were very happy worshiping that way. Nevertheless, they also agreed it might be time to freshen up their song choices with some newer expressions of faith. So they looked forward to the arrival of their new worship leader with guarded anticipation. But what they got was a full frontal assault. He changed everything: the songs, accompaniment, order of worship, volume levels, and everything else that was possibly changeable. A few younger members applauded his assault on the status quo. But the majority of the congregation was shocked and saddened to have their worship turned upside down. Some got angry. Relationships between the worship leader and the people became awkward and forced. Church members reacted with cool nods as they passed him in the church hallways and grocery store aisles. The beleaguered young worship leader sought advice from a pastor who took his own church through such a major change of worship style. The changes this pastor had instigated in his church had come at a high cost, as many had left that church. But the pastor firmly believed that his church was better off without those tired old traditionalists holding them back. He noted that the remnant left behind was worshiping with real feeling, and he was sure many more would be attracted soon to join the church. His attractional rationale, of course, was to get people into church to win the world for Christ. He expected that the remaining remnant would soon see numerical growth since worship was so much better now. So when the young worship leader sought out the pastor's advice it was given authoritatively: "You are the leader; you are in charge; you must make them follow you. And if they fire you, you can always go start a church somewhere else. Don't let them intimidate you. God is in this."

Now, please allow me to ask some tough questions: How is this young worship leader's approach any different from the missionary who forces his home culture on the native people he is called to serve? How can this pastor be so misled as to think that the way to grow the body of Christ in spiritual maturity is to run off a large percentage of the membership? How can either of these men think that their personal preference of worship style is superior to those faithful members who have been there for years? Like those in Babel, we cannot expect to escape the judgment of God if we are building memorials to our own stylistic tastes. The answers seem obvious to me; yet I encounter this situation constantly in my work with churches. I know that a church member who cannot support the stated mission of the pastor is right to find another church. But the notion that we must purify the church of longtime members by forcing a foreign worship culture on them seems ridiculous to me. And I find this especially aggravating if the rationale behind that strategy is: "We'll win the world by getting the world to come to church." Disguised in our worship wars is often a far deadlier enemy than stylistic change for the sake of attracting the world. The hidden enemy in many worship wars is our selfish desire to have our own way and be in control.

What is missing in the above case study? How can we fit our understanding of worship and culture together in a way that glorifies God and takes us full circle? Let's start by reviewing what we know so far in this journey of understanding.

- First, God created worship for himself. Worship is never about us; instead, worship is "all about" God.
- Second, our style preferences are idolatrous when we put them on the throne of worship.
- Third, real worship, empowered by spirit and truth, connects us to God to help us fall deeply in love with him. This love ignites us to a lifetime of daily discipleship and mission.
- Fourth, culture is a tool from God we can use to connect people with him.

Here is my two-fold conclusion. Read it carefully and think about it. It may shake your pre-conceptions:

- Conclusion One—In the Church: Culture should connect Christians to God in their heart language. Worship must be totally focused on God alone. Style in the church exists for no other reason than to connect Christians with God and move them to deeper discipleship and mission. For our church members, we must offer worship in their heart languages to ignite them to daily discipleship and mission action.

- Conclusion Two—In the World: Once Christians have been connected with God in the circle of missional living, God sends us to the world to connect others with him in their heart language. We must learn the unique cultural expressions of our target group so we can communicate the gospel in their indigenous heart language.

There it is, as simple as that. We first worship in our heart language. Then we go learn the heart language of the target group to whom God sends us. With this understanding, our slavery to attractional thinking can be broken. We are free to connect Christians with God in a style that fits them best so that they can be sent on mission. If this means offering different worship services in different styles, then so be it. Meeting people where they are in their heart language to communicate the gospel is the essence of being missional. And if you are afraid of creating different churches within your church, remember that unity comes from a unifying mission, not simply sitting in the same room at the same hour once a week.

So, the deciding factors in providing multiple worship services in your church to meet multiple needs are:

- Spiritual Maturity: If your church's members are spiritually mature enough to sacrifice their own heart languages for others, you can provide only one worship service. Aim the worship style at the majority, but include the wider spectrum of heart languages from time to time.
- Resources: If your church does not have the size or resources to offer more than one service, you can provide only one service and offer as many of your congregation's heart languages as possible in that service. Constantly teach them to focus on God and call them to sacrifice for each other. But beware, you may discover why blended worship is sometimes referred to as "the equal opportunity offender."
- Missional Intent: If your church has the resources, spiritual maturity and missional intent to offer worship in a variety of heart languages, then, by all means, do so. But don't just guess at the heart languages of your congregation. Research and poll them to target their heart languages as closely as possible.

I certainly believe that most of our evangelical churches have the ability and resources to offer different services in different styles. But please remember the most important point in all of this. We must know that the goal of worship is to connect us with God so that we are sent on mission. Worship can never be about us. If we discern our church's heart language simply to meet our own needs and keep us happy, we will have missed God's intent for us as his children.

No more forcing a worship culture on a congregation under the mistaken assumption that it will help win the world for Christ by getting people into church. No more arguing about which style is better. No more worship wars resulting from putting our preference on the throne. What a relief! Simply start where your people are and use their heart language to connect them with God, grow them as disciples, and send them out to join God's mission.

Return to the Cross

All creatures of our God and King,
Lift up your voice and with us sing
Alleluia! Alleluia!
Thou burning sun with golden beam,
Thou silver moon with softer gleam!
O praise him! Alleluia![6]

God has set this world in order. It runs like clockwork in infinite detail with amazing precision. The order of this world testifies to a mastermind of infinite proportions. Yet God's attention to detail extends to the smallest thing. As mankind lives and moves within this infinitely organized world, we organize our own lives as we reflect God's creativity and resourcefulness. We call it culture. And when the cultural organization of our lives is in tune with God, we live in harmony as his creation. But when we assume the role of demi-god and force a foreign culture onto a people, we move outside of God's graceful order. Skirmishes begin to disrupt the grace relationship in which God calls us to live. The joy of singing "Alleluia" is lost when we are under attack from those who should bring God's grace. War breaks out in our soul, in our relationships, and in our churches. The term "worship war" is an oxymoron. There can be no war in worship when worship belongs solely to God.

And all ye men of tender heart,
Forgiving others, take your part,
O sing ye! Alleluia!
Ye who long pain and sorrow bear,
Praise God and on Him cast your care!
O praise him! Alleluia!

6. Francis of Assisi, paraphrased by William Draper and Thomas Ken, "All Creatures of Our God and King," Public Domain.

How can we rediscover the joy of "Alleluia" when the song of heartfelt worship has been drowned out by a worship war? Hearts may once again become tender through praising God and casting our cares on him. Our souls cry out to God in the unique language of our hearts. In those heart languages we embrace the cross and the love given there. May this act of worship bring you to forgive those who have forced their culture on you. Then may you rise in "humbleness" and worship our God with a fresh spirit, free from the hurts of the past. "O praise him. Alleluia!"

Let all things their Creator bless,
And worship him in humbleness,
O praise him! Alleluia!
Praise, praise the Father, praise the Son,
And praise the Spirit, Three in One!
O praise him! O praise him!
Alleluia! Alleluia! Alleluia!

Questions for Thought and Discussion

Name five ways that your daily life expresses the culture that you live in.

Where do you see culture being elevated to the throne of worship in your own life and church?

Describe here your own personal heart language in terms of music, style, language, art, food, and other elements.

How would you analyze/evaluate your own church's worship in terms of the Vital Contextual Worship definition?

Where have you seen or experienced a foreign culture being forced on an existing culture? What feelings were evident from people involved in that experience?

How can you and your church apply conclusion one and conclusion two to move past worship wars and become missional? What are three potential results of putting these two conclusions into action?

Based on the three deciding factors for presenting different worship services to meet different needs, is your own church ready for providing multiple services or adding more services? Why or why not?

12

Missions 101 for Worshipers

Our Missional Viewpoint

> And I will put enmity between you and the woman, and between your offspring and hers; he will crush your head, and you will strike his heel. Genesis 3:15, NIV

A WORLDVIEW IS THE lens through which people view and understand life. In *Basic Training for Mission Teams,* Jerry Rankin and Phyllis Tadlock defined worldview as: "Shared beliefs, feelings and values that drive the behavior and life patterns of individuals and cultures."[1] A Christian worldview sees history as "his story," the story of God's mission to redeem the world. God's story is a continuum with a beginning and an end. Some have portrayed this redemption story as the story of three trees: the tree of good and evil in the Garden of Eden; the tree of Calvary where Jesus gave his life for us; and the tree of life in Revelation 2:7 at the end of this age. In the above Scripture, God unveiled his redemption plan immediately after Adam and Eve fell into sin. God revealed to Satan as serpent that ultimately Jesus would crush his head even after Satan had wounded the Son of Man. This prophecy was fulfilled in Jesus' crucifixion and resurrection.

The Bible is full of stories showing our God on mission to restore fallen humanity. His redemption story unfolds in distinctive chapters across the ages: the creation; the fall into sin; the plan of redemption announced; the faith covenant with Abraham to bless the world through his offspring; the prophecies of the coming of Messiah; the

1. Rankin and Tadlock, *Basic Training for Mission Teams,* 28.

birth, ministry, crucifixion, and victorious resurrection of Jesus Christ; the Great Commissioning of the church to join God on his redemptive mission; the gospel taken to the nations; the second coming of Christ; and the consummation of his story when all disciples are worshiping the Lamb at the heavenly throne.

You and I are a part of this continuing story. We have been commissioned by God to join his mission and share his story. What an amazing concept, that God would use people like us as an integral part of his plan.

Our Missional Eyes

> For God so loved the world that He gave
> His only begotten Son. John 3:16a, KJV

If God were to walk the streets of our cities and towns, what would be his perspective? God would walk our streets with a broken heart looking into each face that did not know him. Relationship with people is the reason God created the earth and placed us on this planet. And God made relationship possible by sending Jesus to die for our sin and conquer spiritual death forever.

So if God walked our streets knowing that he has already made every provision for relationship, his heart would break for those who remain separated from him. Those outside of relationship with God in Christ are dead people walking—fully alive physically, yet dead spiritually. And his heart breaks for each one. Our missional eyes are opened when we understand that our friends, neighbors, and co-workers are spiritually dead without Christ. Our hearts, too, must break for them.

In the past 20 years, the evangelical community began to look at the world differently. Focus shifted to evangelizing people groups rather than nations. The *Basic Training for Mission Teams* manual tells us: "Of the thousands of people groups worldwide, about 4,992 people groups live in the Last Frontier—the part of the world with little or no access to the gospel. That translates to 1.6 billion people who currently have virtually no chance of hearing the good news of Jesus Christ."[2] As we can readily see, God is on mission to win both our own communities and those who have never heard the gospel. He is calling us to join him in all those places.

2. Rankin and Tadlock, *Basic Training for Mission Teams*, 51.

Our Missional Heart

> And this is the testimony: God has given us eternal life, and this life is in his Son. He who has the Son has life; he who does not have the Son of God does not have life. I write these things to you who believe in the name of the Son of God, so that you may know that you have eternal life.
> 1 John 5:11–13, NIV

From time to time, both personally and with evangelistic teams, I have had the privilege of hitting the streets to talk to people about Christ. Street witnessing is evangelism, a part of the larger whole of missions, and very valuable in planting gospel seeds in lives. We often use a simple evangelistic tract made to look like a million dollar bill (www.livingwaters.com/store/tracts). Printed on the back of the million dollar bill is a concise presentation of the gospel. "Have you gotten your million dollar bill today?" we ask as someone approaches. Some will say, "I'm not interested," and walk on, but most are intrigued and will say, "Wow, is that real? Can I have it?"

"Yes," is the reply, "but you have to answer the million-dollar question. The question is this: 'If you die tonight, how will you convince God to let you into heaven?'"

The great majority of people will answer, "Well, I am trying my best to live a good life and do right. I hope God will let me in."

If this is your response, you are dead wrong. The Scripture from 1 John gives us the one and only key to spiritual life. Far too many people in our churches and out on the streets just don't understand. They somehow think that the power to reach up to God depends on their own effort. No matter how much you try, attempting to live good enough to earn heaven is a dead-end road. If you think you should go on mission to earn God's favor, forget it. If you have never opened your life to Christ, do it now! Stop right here and ask Christ to come into your heart as your eternal King, Lord, and Savior.

Our Missional Mind

> I, the Lord, have called you for a righteous purpose, and I will hold you by your hand. I will keep you, and I will make you a covenant for the people and a light to the nations, in order to open blind eyes, to bring out prisoners from the dungeon, and those sitting in darkness from the prison house. I am Yahweh, that is My name. Isaiah 42:6–8a, HCSB

Mission is the work of God to reconcile our sinful world to himself, and it is eternally rooted in his own will and nature: God originated the mission; Jesus Christ enacted the mission; the Holy Spirit empowers the mission; the church carries out missions; we tell the world the good news of reconciliation through Jesus; a person accepts Jesus Christ as Savior and Lord, becomes a disciple, and joins God's mission. God's love goes full circle in missions. John Piper, in *Let the Nations Be Glad,*[3] wrote, "When this age is over, and the countless millions of the redeemed fall on their faces before the throne of God, missions will be no more. It is a temporary necessity."

Gailyn Van Rheenen, in *Missions: Biblical Foundations and Contemporary Strategies,*[4] pointed out that there are at least five things that Christians must understand when we join God's mission: "First, if mission flows from the character and nature of God, it cannot be neglected by the church. Mission, because it is of God, cannot be aborted. Second, since the mission is of God, God will equip people for the task. If they feel inadequate, he will empower them. Third, the mission of God enables Christian missionaries to understand themselves under God's sovereignty. Christians should not undertake God's mission for self-glorification but for the glorification of God. It is God's enterprise. Fourth, the mission of God implies sacrifice. It is a mission worth living and dying for. Finally, because the mission is God's, it will succeed. Even though messengers fail and people reject the message, the mission of God continues. God, the source of mission, will raise up new people to carry his message."

Understanding these five things about missions will help you clarify your role in the mission of God. How many of our church members, or our pastors for that matter, can clearly put into words the mission of God and our work of missions? We are quick to tell anyone what we think our church should be. But our church wish-list seldom mirrors God's mission in the world.

3. Piper, *Let the Nations Be Glad,* page unknown.
4. Van Rheenen, *Missions: Biblical Foundations and Contemporary Strategies,* 19.

Our Mission Message

> But you are a chosen people, a royal priesthood, a holy nation, a people belonging to God, that you may declare the praises of Him who called you out of darkness into his wonderful light. 1 Peter 2:9, NIV

A 2012 study by LifeWay Research asked Protestant pastors and church members to respond to the statement: "If a person is sincerely seeking God, he/she can obtain eternal life through religions other than Christianity." The alarming statistic is that 12 percent of Protestant pastors actually agreed with the statement. This means that more than 1 in 10 of the responding pastors does not believe that Jesus is the only way to eternal life. Statistics for adults who attend Protestant churches are far more alarming. A startling 26 percent agreed with the statement. That's more than 1 in 4 Protestant church members polled who don't believe Jesus is the only way to God.[5]

The Scriptures call Christians to be a distinctive people. But many Christians today want to look and act like the world to increase our acceptance by the world. Distinctiveness is not something we seem to value as Christians these days. Let's consider this issue in two parts.

First, the message of the gospel calls Christians to a distinctive belief. Without a distinct message, it is almost impossible for the church to call unbelievers into relationship with God. When we believe that other religions lead to eternal life, the message of Christ and the call to God's mission of reconciliation go out the window. Any talk-show host or positive-thinking guru can piece together a message from world religions that makes us feel good. American society tells us, "Co-exist! Live, and let live. Lifestyles are in, religion is out. Everybody has a right to embrace their own belief system. There is no right and wrong as long as you don't hurt someone or their things."

But God calls his people to boldly proclaim Christ as God's singular means of reconciliation. Will we listen to our God or to our world?

Jesus said himself, "I am the way and the truth and the life. No one comes to the Father except through me" (John 14:6, NIV). Mohammed specifically says in the Koran that Jesus is not God. Jewish faith says that the Son of God, the Messiah, has not yet come. Buddhism says that there is no God. Hinduism says there are many gods. These religions are mutually exclusive. You can't get around that fact. We must offer the world the only thing that will make a difference. Offer them the real truth of God. God

5. Roach, "Pastors Uphold Christian Exclusivity Poll Finds," www.lifeway.com.

designed us to be incomplete without him. He completes us for eternal life exclusively through his only son Jesus. There is no other way to God.

Second, the message of the gospel calls Christians to a distinctive lifestyle. Without a distinctive lifestyle, it is almost impossible for the church to call unbelievers to relationship with God. If our behavior is no different from those around us, how can we tell them that Christ will make a difference in their lives? As discussed in chapter 8, God expects his followers to consistently exhibit the fruit of the Spirit: love, joy, peace, patience, kindness, goodness, faithfulness, gentleness, and self-control. If these qualities do not signify our lives, how can we be significant in pointing others to God? Our distinctive lifestyle must be a bright beacon to our neighbors, co-workers, and friends.

Our Missional Face

> Have this attitude in yourselves which was also in Christ Jesus, who, although he existed in the form of God, did not regard equality with God a thing to be grasped, but emptied himself, taking the form of a bond-servant, and being made in the likeness of men. Philippians 2: 6–7, NASB

The operative word in missions is "incarnation." John 1:14 (HCSB) says, "The Word became flesh and took up residence among us." Incarnate means "in bodily form." Jesus brought God's Word to life, in the flesh. As disciples on mission, we bring the gospel to life, in the flesh. In their manual *Launching Missional Communities: A Field Guide*, Mike Breen and Alex Absalom define incarnational as: "changing our message from 'come to us and look like us' to 'we're coming to you and showing you Christ where you are.'"[6]

As stated in previous chapters, my definition of missions has become "meeting people at their point of need on a regular basis in your community to build relationships which lead to witnessing opportunities." Across the past 30 years in the evangelical church, we have emphasized that every church member is a minister, not just the paid staff. But the Bible calls every church member to be a missionary, too. When we incarnate the gospel to the world, ministry will happen alongside missions. Just as Christ became love in the flesh, so must we. The greatest Christian mission force in the

6. Breen and Absalom, *Launching Missional Communities: A Field Guide*, 28.

world is sitting inside our churches. Break out, church; go embody Christ to your community!

Our Missional Strategy

> They said, "Cornelius, a centurion, an upright and God-fearing man, who has a good reputation with the whole Jewish nation, was divinely directed by a holy angel to call you to his house and to hear a message from you." The following day he (Peter) entered Caesarea. Now Cornelius was expecting them and had called together his relatives and close friends. Acts 10:22, 24, HCSB

Here is the goal of missions: That a year from now, there would be more people who know Christ as Savior, as a percentage of the population of a specific people group, than right now. Based on that specific goal, we must "develop a contextual process to reach, disciple, congregationalize (gather), mobilize, and reproduce believers among specific ethnic, lifestyle and life-stage groups," a definition of missional strategy that Curt Watke teaches in his missional training.[7]

Across America and the world, new strategies are springing up almost daily to accomplish this goal. My purpose is not to recommend one or the other, but rather to encourage us to explore the variety of ways God is moving to win people. The establishment of missional communities is one such strategy sweeping our world. Reggie McNeal accurately chronicles these in his book *Missional Communities: The Rise of the Post-Congregational Church.* McNeal is careful to say that missional communities can exist alongside our congregational churches as an alternative church life form. And both can and must learn from each other. The term "missional community" embraces a wide variety of groups. In general they are groups of between ten and seventy people collaborating together to fulfill a mission strategy. Sometimes, a missional community is formed by smaller cluster groups such as discipleship groups, etc. Members of missional communities worship, study, grow and do missions together in formal and informal ways. 3DM Ministries, founded by Mike Breen, facilitates missional communities to model the three dimensions of Up-In-Out. This is a close correlation to the full circle of worship-discipleship-mission. I highly recommend *Launching Missional Communities: A*

7. Watke, "M3 lectures." South Carolina Baptist Convention, 2012–2013, used with permission.

Field Guide by Mike Breen and Alex Absalom for excellent insight into missional communities and how they function. This resource is based on more than 20 years of developing a practical nuts-and-bolts approach to starting highly effective missional communities.

The house church is one prevalent form of missional community. Since New Testament days, the house church has been a powerful seed in church planting. The house church movement is alive and well across the world, moving under the radar of institutional awareness and control. House churches are the engine fueling the rapid growth of Christianity in China, India, Brazil, and many other parts of the world. Lessons from the house church movement—both good and bad—can give excellent insight into leading your worship ministry to become a missional community. You can read more about the house church network at http://housechurch.org/about.html.

Meanwhile, institutional churches are being revitalized by the "mission outpost" strategy. An outpost mission team is called out and trained in the five-fingered-approach specifically to start mission outposts to become new churches under the guidance of the sponsoring church. The mission outpost process is very simple: form and train a mission team, target a people group in your community, place the team at a home or public setting to do missions, form a home discipleship group from contacts made there, and then grow the discipleship group into a house church to reach indigenous people around them.

These strategies and many more are predicated upon finding the "person of peace" and his/her household. In Luke 10:5–7 (NIV), Jesus sent his disciples on mission with this instruction: "When you enter a house, first say, 'Peace to this house.' If someone who promotes peace is there, your peace will rest on them; if not, it will return to you. Stay there, eating and drinking whatever they give you, for the worker deserves his wages. Do not move around from house to house."

God shows us where he is about to visit by the presence of one or more people of peace. In the Scripture above we see Cornelius, the person of peace who reached out to Peter and opened his household. God instructs us to look for a person of peace in a target people group and connect with that person and his/her household. If there is no person of peace there, then we simply move on. God may prepare the most unlikely people to be your "person(s) of peace," so be open to everyone. Finding and building a relationship with the person(s) of peace is the key to connecting with their households—their relational networks. It is imperative to involve persons of peace in our missional communities as quickly as possible so they embrace the gospel and join God's mission. This will equip them to be leaders as our outpost grows into an indigenous church or missional community on its own.

So here is the circle of missional strategy:

1. Churches present local mission events;
2. From those events, mission outposts are established to meet people at their point of need on a regular basis in your community through ongoing mission projects;
3. Persons of peace are discovered from the mission outposts and enlisted to host Bible storying groups in their home or another community setting;
4. As people in the group accept Jesus as Savior, the outposts become indigenous house churches;
5. House churches link together to become a constituted church or missional community;
6. These present local mission events . . . and the missional strategy keeps going full circle.

New Testament churches were basically missional communities worshiping, discipling, and doing missions. They reached out to persons of peace in their own communities and established new missional communities household to household. Using this model, Christianity grew exponentially in three centuries from about 1,000 believers in 40 A.D. to 33.8 million by 350 A.D. Would you agree that the strategy worked? Can the strategy work today? I am challenging our worship ministries to become missional communities, discovering persons of peace in their neighborhoods, and discipling them to establish mission outposts for the sharing of the gospel of our Savior and Lord, Jesus Christ.

Our Missional Music

> Now while Paul was waiting for them at Athens, his spirit was being provoked within him as he was observing the city full of idols. So he was reasoning in the synagogue with the Jews and the God-fearing Gentiles, and in the market place every day with those who happened to be present. And also some of the Epicurean and Stoic philosophers were conversing with him. Acts 17:16–18, NASB

Ethnomusicology is the comparative study of music from different cultures. Ethnomusicologists combine the study of musicology with anthropology to analyze music as a reflection of society and culture. Missional ethnomusicologists encourage the development of indigenous Christian songs produced by the local believers in their own language and music system. Music workshops are presented to native peoples illustrating the value of using local music systems rather than foreign systems, thinking through Scripture passages that might be put to music, composing new Christian songs in their own native style, and recording the new songs. In this way, the gospel becomes incarnate in the musical language of the native people.

A Brazilian missionary reported that a Palikur woman was asked, "Which do you like better, the hymns with non-Indian music, or the ones with the Palikur tunes."

She replied, "We like them both, but the ones with our music can make us cry."

Using the heart music of a people connects the gospel with their own legacy. Missionaries have reported that native people, normally apathetic about Christianity, listened with great attention to the words of new Christian songs written by their own musicians in their own style. Putting the biblical message in an indigenous style gives it an authority it would not otherwise have. We, too, must be ethnomusicologists. Worship leaders need to analyze their communities to effectively connect them with God in their indigenous cultures.

Paul was very careful to analyze the surrounding cultural context wherever he went. In the above Scripture, we see him relating to Jews in the synagogue, to Athenian citizens in the marketplace, and to Greek philosophers. In every one of those contexts, Paul saw idolatry alive and well. As a missionary, each of us must analyze our context as well. Who are the people groups in your community/town/city? And what are the idols they have substituted for relationship with almighty God?

The Intercultural Institute for Contextual Ministry offers many resources on its website, www.iicm.net, for analyzing the ethno-musical context of our communities. First, we must know the classifications and characteristics of people groups in general before we can analyze who is in our community. IICM identifies these American communities:

- Upscale Communities. Affluent families living primarily in suburbia but also in posh neighborhoods in urban settings.

- Mainstay Communities. A diverse mix of ethnically mixed singles, couples, and families in established, diverse neighborhoods within small towns and second cities.
- Working Communities. Racially-mixed, lower middle-class blue-collar households living in older towns.
- Country Communities. Rural families with outdoor-oriented life-styles working in agricultural and mining communities.
- Aspiring Communities. An eclectic group of young, mostly single, ethnically-diverse households living in homes, apartments, and group quarters.
- Urban Communities. Ethnically-diverse singles and single-parent renters living in struggling-diverse, inner-city neighborhoods.

Using these socio-economic classifications for community analysis, IICM gathers data from a variety of sources including the most recent government census, Arbitron radio ratings, and sales-tracking data to give us insights about a particular cultural context. According to the 2011 Arbitron radio ratings, here is what each of these communities were listening to by percentage of radio market:

Radio Type	Upscale	Mainstay	Working	Country	Aspiring	Urban
Adult Contemporary	22.66%	*18.77%	18.35%	*17.74%	14.42%	11.59%
Adult Standards	3.41%	4.49%	2.92%	2.17%	3.62%	1.15%
Gospel	1.09%	0.99%	1.48%	3.07%	4.33%	4.48%
Contempo-rary Hit Radio	18.21%	18.34%	*21.63%	13.48%	*21.71%	*19.80%
Classic Rock	13.86%	11.18%	11.56%	6.55%	5.78%	10.71%
Classical	5.89%	3.39%	2.35%	1.75%	4.50%	1.88%
Country	*18.25%	24.89%	25.63%	44.45%	10.52%	13.58%
Jazz	4.75%	4.03%	1.75%	0.63%	10.24%	4.49%
Oldies	13.54%	10.80%	11.31%	9.97%	8.36%	9.82%
Soft Contemporary	9.09%	7.23%	4.29%	2.81%	5.47%	4.14%
Urban Contemporary	7.04%	8.14%	7.95%	4.71%	26.66%	27.96%
Variety	9.83%	8.91%	8.03%	5.45%	12.65%	11.08%

Radio Type	Upscale	Mainstay	Working	Country	Aspiring	Urban
Alternative	15.03%	8.65%	8.32%	4.77%	7.92%	4.92%
Classic Hits	4.92%	4.46%	4.59%	2.68%	2.52%	1.78%
Easy Listening	0.76%	1.11%	0.74%	0.26%	0.17%	0.17%
Rock	13.97%	11.90%	13.97%	9.37%	8.38%	6.09%

Obviously, this data is limited: first, it is dated from 2011; second, it only includes radio listening habits and does not include data from personal listening devices. But despite those limitations it remains useful for analysis of general music trends in our American communities.

In the chart above, I have underlined the most popular radio category for each community type and added a star to the second most popular. Churches far and wide have started contemporary services using popular musical styles that they suppose will connect their members with God and be attractive to the world. Such Christian writers as Chris Tomlin, Tommy Walker, Laura Storey, and Paul Baloche, as well as a multitude of others, have given us wonderful songs of worship. Their songs are in a pop style that relates to those who listen to Adult Contemporary radio. But that's where this strategy breaks down, and here's why. The Arbitron ratings show clearly that the leading radio style is Country music in Mainstay, Working, and Country communities. Urban Contemporary music, which includes rap and hip-hop, is the leading style in two communities —Aspiring and Urban—while Contemporary Hit radio leads only in Upscale communities.

The style of music being used in most contemporary worship services best compares with Adult Contemporary secular radio. If we are going to effectively connect all people with God, we must offer worship in other musical heart languages as well. Yet how many churches do you know that are offering a worship service featuring country, rap and hip-hop, top forty, or the myriad of other styles available? Can we truly think we are connecting all worshippers with God when only contemporary and traditional styles are being offered on any given Sunday?

Our "blended" worship, too, is often restricted to a blend of only contemporary and traditional church styles. A true blend will be more representative of the musical heart languages of our church when we include all musical styles prevalent in our community. I believe, however, that worship is more effective offering different styles in multiple services wherever believers differ in their musical heart language, as opposed to simply offering a blended service. This enables traditional worshipers to continue to embrace the hymnody of the past while other groups embrace styles that resonate with them. Radio stations understand that blending seldom works. Top forty stations don't offer a daily classical symphony; country stations don't suddenly break in with a few jazz selections, and rap stations don't program an occasional hour of contemporary adult hits and oldies.

So if we are going to truly connect our people with God in deeper discipleship and active missions, we must know our church's heart languages. Too often we assume we know our people and their favorite styles of expression. One thing the radio preference chart shows us is that we probably don't even know what they are listening to on their way home from church. It is dangerous to assume we are on target with our worship planning and are speaking their cultural language without researching it. Or worse, we are arrogant if we think we know what is best for them and what style God prefers.

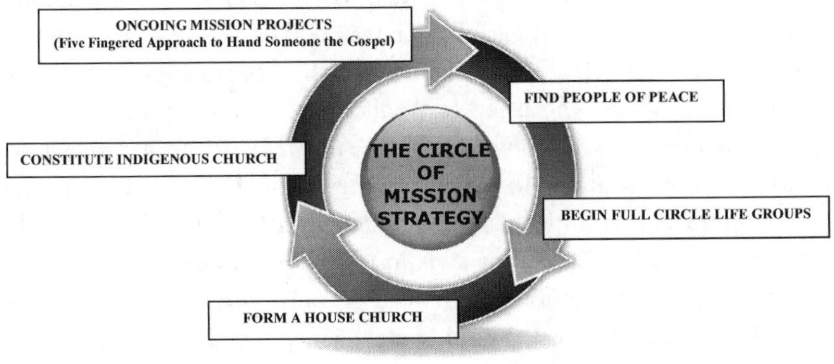

Diagram 5

Return to the Cross

I stand amazed in the presence of Jesus the Nazarene,
and wonder how He could love me, a sinner condemned unclean.
How marvelous, how wonderful, and my song shall ever be:
How marvelous, how wonderful is my Savior's love for me.[8]

Jesus had sent his disciples on mission. They had returned to recount gloriously of the miracles they had performed and lives they had touched in Jesus' name. What an amazing privilege was theirs to be in Jesus' presence

8. Gabriel, "I Stand Amazed in the Presence," Public Domain.

everyday and see his love touching lives. And when Jesus asked Peter his opinion of who Jesus is, Peter replied, "You are the messiah of God." Jesus didn't deny it. What must the disciples have thought? These Jewish men, looking for a conquering messiah to restore the kingdom of Israel to power and sovereignty, must have thought, "Our time has come. Surely God will vindicate his chosen nation now and we will rule with him, sitting at his right hand."

He took my sins and my sorrows,
He made them His very own.
He bore my burden to Calvary and suffered and died alone.
How marvelous, how wonderful, and my song shall ever be:
How marvelous, how wonderful is my Savior's love for me.

Immediately after Peter's confession, Jesus drastically reoriented the disciples' thinking. First, he foretold his own crucifixion. Then he gave them two commands: deny yourself and take up the cross. A shudder of fear must have chilled them as they heard Jesus' reference to the cross—the Roman instrument of torture and death reserved for the worst criminals. If my Savior is to bear rejection and death for others, then I as his disciple must follow the same path of service. In one sentence, Christ redefined what it means to follow him. The essence of kingdom living is now self-denial and service, not power or coercion. Take up the cross and follow Christ in self-sacrifice!

When with the ransomed in glory, His face I at last shall see,
Twill be my song through the ages to sing of His love for me.
How marvelous, how wonderful, and my song shall ever be:
How marvelous, how wonderful is my Savior's love for me.

Questions for Thought and Discussion

Write a phrase explaining each of these in your own words.

- Our Missional Viewpoint:
- Our Missional Eyes:
- Our Missional Heart:
- Our Missional Mind:
- Our Missional Message:
- Our Missional Face:

- Our Missional Strategy:
- Our Missional Music:

How can your worship team become a missional community to fulfill a missions strategy?

Define the person of peace.

Who would be a person of peace that you have known or have heard of?

In which community type would you place your household? In what community types would you place your relational network?

Do your household and network conform to the musical preference chart presented in this chapter?

How can your worship ministry use Missions 101 to better connect your church with God for deeper discipleship and sending into missions?

13

Leading Through Change to Action

> Can the Ethiopian change his skin or the leopard its spots? Neither can you do good who are accustomed to doing evil. Jeremiah 13:23, NIV

In the cover article entitled "Change or Die" for *Fast Company* magazine, May 2005 edition, Alan Deutschman posed the question, "If you were told today that you must make significant changes in your lifestyle or face imminent death, could you make the necessary changes? Yes, you say? Try again. *Yes?* You're probably deluding yourself. Here are the odds, the scientifically studied odds: nine to one. That's nine to one against you. How do you like those odds?"[1]

Deutschman reported that in 2005, at IBM's Global Outlook Conference, a panel of experts was enlisted to study the American healthcare crisis. Healthcare at that time was consuming an astounding 15 percent of our Gross National Product at 1.8 trillion dollars a year. As the dream team of experts took the stage, everyone held their breath in anticipation of a breakthrough. What was the answer from their exhaustive research?

Ray Levey, founder of the Global Medical Forum, told the audience, "A relatively small percentage of the population consumes the vast majority of the health-care budget for diseases that are very well known and are by and large behavioral."[2]

Edward Miller, dean of the medical school and CEO at Johns Hopkins University Hospital, continued the report: "If you look at people after coronary artery bypass, ninety percent of them have not changed their lifestyle.

1. Deutschman, "Change or Die," *Fast Company*, page unknown.
2. Ibid.

That's been studied over and over again. Even though they know they have a very bad disease and they know they should change their lifestyle, for whatever reason, they can't."[3]

In other words, most of us are sick because we refuse to change our basic behavior to get well. When faced with the choice to change or die, nine out of ten of us refuse to change. In fact, the panel discovered that CEOs, supposedly the primary change agents for their companies, are often as resistant to change as anyone and as prone to backsliding. Do you think that might also be true for church leaders?

What set apart the 10 percent of heart patients who embraced change from the 90 percent who rejected it? The answer gives us some important insights into motivating change. Deutschman cited John Kotter, a Harvard Business School professor who studied dozens of organizations in the midst of upheaval: "The central issue is never strategy, structure, culture, or systems. The core of the matter is always about changing the behavior of people . . . Behavioral change happens most effectively by speaking to people's feelings. In highly successful change efforts, people find ways to help others see the problems or solutions in ways that influence emotions, not just thought."[4]

The ability to manage change will always depend on the quality of your relationships. Remember, Christianity is foremost a relationship with God through Christ, not a religion. So resolve to build relationships ever deeper as the context for your leadership. Then, in the context of relationship, influence the emotions of worshipers to embrace change by:

1. Asking powerful questions. We can move worshipers emotionally by asking them leading questions. Good questions first help them identify the emotional issues blocking their objectivity. Next, questions can lead them to discover missional solutions they can embrace. Finally, your questions should move them toward personal commitment to spiritual growth. Transition your relational methodology from providing answers to asking questions that motivate change.

2. Using the storying method. Storying blazes a trail through our emotions to our intellect. Bible storying connects our heart with God by speaking to our feelings. That's why Jesus taught the crowds in parables.

3. Ibid.
4. Ibid.

3. Sharing powerful missional stories. Real life stories are an effective way to inspire change. Present the problems first and then tell the success stories of those finding missional solutions to problems in your community.

Leaders today must find new ways to reach people's hearts to affect life-change. Leadership specialists like Reggie McNeal are helping us see that true leaders first sell the problem before they sell the solution. Present the problems in ways that move us emotionally and challenge our hearts. Changed hearts lead to changed people. Changed people can change churches and our world.

> Are you tired? Worn out? Burned out on religion? Come to me. Get away with me and you'll recover your life. I'll show you how to take a real rest. Walk with me and work with me—watch how I do it. Learn the unforced rhythms of grace. I won't lay anything heavy or ill-fitting on you. Keep company with me. You'll learn to live freely and lightly. Matthew 11:28–30, The Message

Dictionary.com defines change as: "1. to make the form, nature, content, future course, etc., of something different from what it is, or from what it would be if left alone; 2. to transform or convert."[5]

An unknown writer said: "I cannot say whether things will get better if we change; what I can say is that they must change if they are to get better."

Socrates said: "Let him who would change the world first change himself."

The Bible talks about change, too. Most Scriptures using the word "change" are assurances that God's nature will remain unchanged throughout eternity. The remaining Scriptures mentioning change are commands to change our lives to align with God. Though God's nature never changes, the world he created is ever-changing. Change is a naturally occurring result of a dynamic universe made by a creative God. So we must learn to lead through change because change is always going to be a part of life.

The Scripture above is the key to unlock God's plan for leading through change. God is the real leader, and we are following him. Henry and Richard Blackaby, in their book, *Spiritual Leadership: Moving People on to God's Agenda*, wrote: "The key to spiritual leadership is for leaders to

5. www.dictionary.com.

understand God's will for them and their organizations. They then move people away from their own agendas and on to God's."[6]

The Scripture in Matthew 11 tells us to "walk, work, and watch" in God, so we will "learn the unforced rhythms of grace." A leader must stay so close to God that we hear his whisper and walk in his shadow. There is no guarantee that this level of trust and obedience will bring success in worldly terms. Jesus lived like this, and it took him to the cross. Yet we trust in the power of the resurrection regardless of the sacrifice it takes to get there.

> One of my brothers, came from Judah with some other men . . . They said to me, "Those who survived the exile and are back in the province are in great trouble and disgrace. The wall of Jerusalem is broken down, and its gates have been burned with fire." Nehemiah 1:1–3, NIV

We dream of doing great things for God. But dreams only become reality through a persistent commitment to a process that produces results. Without a plan that yields results, our greatest dreams remain unrealized. Artistic people seem to have no shortage of dreams. But artistic people sometimes struggle to develop and follow a strategic plan. Creating an artistic masterpiece requires a disciplined approach. Here is the process you can follow to create a missional masterpiece.

Step one: Seek God and his vision

> When I heard these things, I sat down and wept. For some days I mourned and fasted and prayed before the God of heaven. Nehemiah 1:4 NIV

God is at work restoring his own masterpiece in this world. He wants to inspire you to join him in his mission. The word "inspiration" literally means "breathed into." From within, the Holy Spirit calls us and empowers us for the mission. Remember, the statistics show us that we can't change ourselves. Only a God-given vision has a chance of success. Only God can lead you through change to action. Surrender your will to him—seek him, find him and follow him.

6. Blackaby and Blackaby, *Spiritual Leadership: Moving People on to God's Agenda*, 41.

Nehemiah got alone with God, crying out for God to give him a vision. First, he allowed the problem at hand to become personal to him. He became so convicted that he mourned and wept. Then he sought God's solution through prayer and fasting. We must seek the vision God has for us with every fiber of our being.

Step two: Accept the vision and define its form

> Then I prayed to the God of heaven . . . "If it pleases the king and if your servant has found favor in his sight, let him send me to the city in Judah where my fathers are buried so that I can rebuild it." Nehemiah 2:4, NIV

Artists understand form. A work of art is expressed in form, whether it is dance, visual art, sculpture, or any other artistic medium. In music, form is the overarching pattern through which melodies, harmonies, and rhythms are stated and developed. So, too, a missional vision needs form to be stated and developed.

When the hand of God rests on you, he will give you a vision. Nehemiah saw the need, received God's vision, and set out to develop a form. Nehemiah's vision to restore his heritage took on the form of rebuilding Jerusalem. He visited Jerusalem, personally surveyed the destruction, and then formed a mental picture and a verbal description of a rebuilt city. Put your vision in written form.

Step three: Enlist pastor support

> Then the king, with the queen sitting beside him, asked me, "How long will your journey take, and when will you get back?" It pleased the king to send me; so I set a time. Nehemiah 2:6

Nehemiah sought support from his king to pursue the vision. A worship minister must receive the support of his senior pastor to pursue the missional vision. First, find ways to mention your vision in casual conversation, written memos, staff meetings, and face-to-face appointments. Charles Billingsley, worship leader with Jerry Falwell and David Jeremiah, refers to what he calls "the law of the seventh mentioning." He believes we can plan on having to mention an idea at least seven times before it will appear on the radar of our pastor.

Attitude is crucial in the process of asking for endorsement and support from your pastor. This requires much prayer. Don't rush into this meeting. Don't let your excitement make you hurry. Set aside a week or two to pray. Ask God to shape your vision to match the vision of your pastor and vice versa. Your vision must be fused into your pastor's vision for the church. Like a gardener who grafts a branch onto the main vine, you want your vision to enhance the pastor's greater vision for the church.

When you have a sense of peace and confidence in the Lord, schedule a meeting with your pastor. Trust God to do his work between you. Begin by asking your pastor to share his overarching vision with you. We trust that the heart of every Christian executive is to fulfill Christ's Great Commission. But he can express that in many different ways depending on his giftedness, personality, calling, and situation. He may say his vision is organizational unity, or financial security, or numerical growth. Continue to trust God's Spirit no matter what your pastor expresses as a vision.

Your next question is crucial, asked in all sincerity: "How can I help you achieve this vision?" This discussion must be a sharing of hearts and not a sales presentation. Once you have heard their heart on this matter, then share the vision God has placed in your heart. If you are open and adaptable, God will shape your vision through the discussion with your pastor. You may leave the meeting with a different perspective on your vision and how to bring it to reality. But if you have soaked the meeting in prayer, you can trust that God had a hand in forging your vision through this meeting.

If the initial answer is "No," don't despair or give up. Ask permission to re-design and re-define your vision, then ask permission to come back and talk some more. If your pastor accepts your vision and pledges his support, schedule a follow-up appointment to present your written vision statement, smart goals, and action plans.

A prominent worship leader who has successfully served his church for more than 20 years told me, "In pastoral relationships, there are no win-lose situations."

I asked him what he meant. "Any staff member is wrong to ever think he or she will win by making the pastor lose. If your pastor loses, you will lose. If you make sure the pastor wins, you will win, too," he explained.[7]

Here are three actions to make sure your pastor wins as you pursue your vision:

- Pastors need to trust you. They want to know who, what, when, where and why before trusting you. Using smart goals and action plans will help you earn trust.
- Pastors value unity. Your ability to keep people unified while successfully fulfilling the mission is a valuable trait. Your pastor and your church will value you for it.
- Pastors don't like surprises. Make every attempt to keep your pastor informed by copying important documents and correspondence to him. Schedule regular updates in person. Share and celebrate victories and always communicate immediately if problems arise.

Step four: Enlist the mission team

> I also said to him, "If it pleases the king, may I have letters to the governors . . . that they will provide me safe-conduct. . . ? And may I have a letter to Asaph, so he will give me timber. . . ?"
> Nehemiah 2:7–8a, NIV

When God gave me the vision to start M3, the MusicArts Mission Movement among our South Carolina Baptist churches, I prepared to send out invitations to key worship leaders. My goal was to recruit six young worship leaders to join me in igniting the movement. But during the month I planned to send invitations, my father became ill and entered the hospital. Three weeks later God took my dad to heaven. Heartbroken, I was ready to delay the whole M3 process. My supervisor convinced me to send out a general e-mail anyway just to see what interest there might be. Within one week, I had six colleagues signed up and ready to jump aboard. God had already spoken to their hearts and enlisted them by the power of his Spirit. I simply needed to believe and obey God's leadership.

7. Steve Phillips, Music Minister, First Baptist Church, Columbia, S.C., personal conversation.

The vision given to Nehemiah to rebuild the wall of Jerusalem must have seemed impossible. But God's visions are uniquely designed for the one to whom they are given. God will not give you a vision without giving you the innate abilities to complete the task. God will also place around you the resources needed to fulfill the vision. Be open, nevertheless, to sharpening your leadership skills if God leads you to do so.

Make a list of candidates to serve on your mission leadership team and then approach them to share your vision. This step should occur during step two of the discipleship process explained in the next chapter. Help them see and understand the problems: the world is dying without Christ; churches are in decline; few Christians are being discipled and sent on mission for Christ. Then share your vision with them. Most importantly, express what you expect they will receive personally from their involvement. Share success stories and testimonies if you have them. All of us have a longing to be part of something with eternal significance. Appeal to that longing in them. Make sure that they understand that you are recruiting them for a limited time to accomplish a specific task. Few will sign on for unlimited service with no ending point in sight. Then step back and see how God moves in their hearts.

Remember that you cannot program people to respond positively to your vision or mission. Trust God to "call out the called" as he works in those he has chosen to join the mission. Do not take a "no" answer personally. Communicate your vision clearly and enthusiastically and then wait to see who God brings alongside you.

Step five: Create a detailed strategy

> Then I said to them, "You see the trouble we are in: Jerusalem lies in ruins, and its gates have been burned with fire. Come, let us rebuild the wall of Jerusalem, and we will no longer be in disgrace." I also told them about the gracious hand of my God upon me and what the king had said to me. They replied, "Let us start rebuilding." Nehemiah 2:17–18, NIV

Gather those who respond positively. People tend to support what they help create. In your first meeting, involve your leadership team in seeing the missional vision and creating a plan. Here are three necessary steps in this written process:

1. Write a vision statement

A vision statement is a verbal snapshot of the dream God has given you. Leadership gurus will direct you to write a mission statement before you write a vision statement. But our mission has already been given to us in the Great Commission: to grow worshiping disciples on mission. How has God called you to fulfill that mission in your community? Answer with a compelling statement in dynamic language to give the best possible word picture of the vision.

2. Develop SMART goals.

Goal-setting is a must if you are going to achieve your vision. When it comes to setting goals, our normal pattern of life tends to be: I set unreachable goals; I procrastinate and then self-criticize; pressure builds inside and outside of me as I fail to work toward my vision; I abandon the vision and go back to living the same old way. New Year's resolutions seldom work because they follow this pattern. We must be smarter when we set goals to achieve our vision. Developing SMART goals is the smart way to lead through change into action. SMART goals fulfill this acrostic: S = Specific; M = Measurable; A = Attainable; R = Relevant; T = Time Specific.[8]

3. Win with action plans.

An old cliché says: "Failing to plan is planning to fail." Did you know that wasting 30 minutes a day will add up to 11 days wasted every year? You could use those extra 11 days to lead a mission project this year. As you pursue your smart goals, continually ask, "What's important now?" and then, "What's important next?" Your answers to those two questions will help form your action plans.

Here is a worksheet to help the team develop a detailed strategy:

Develop your Mission Vision Statement.

From (month/year)__________ to ____________, I will lead my worship ministry to "meet people at their point of need in our community on a regular basis to build relationships that lead to witnessing opportunities" by doing these things: ______________________________

____

____

8. Doran, Miller, and Cunningham, "There's a S.M.A.R.T. way to write management goals and objectives," *Management Review.* Volume 70, Issue 11, 35–36.

Develop a SMART Goal (Specific/Measurable/Attainable/ Relevant/Time Specific).

I will lead my worship team to present a mission project in my community at the location of______ ________________________, on these dates ___________________________________, using the artistic medium of___________________________________. Our goal is to have a total of______ people participate at least once from the community. We hope to have an average weekly attendance of ______ with whom we will build relationships. We will present the gospel to them in these ways_
____
_____________.

We pray that _____ people will accept Christ as Lord and Savior.

Develop an Action Plan to WIN (What's Important Now? What's Important Next?).

Resources Needed?

____

____

Candidates for Mission Team Members?

____

____

Permissions Needed?

____

____

Training Needed for Team?

____

____

Commit to Lead; Commit to Go.

I covenant with God to join him on his mission to redeem the world. I understand that his plan to accomplish this mission is not to get the world into church, but to get the church into the world. I hereby commit to lead my worship ministry to go to our community with the gospel through the above project. Signed: ___________________________________

Share e-mail addresses and phone numbers to facilitate communication within the team. Pray around the table and dismiss.

Between the first and second meetings, be sure to use the email contact list to accomplish these things:

- Set up the private group blog, social network site, email group or phone list for the team.
- Use a tool such as a D.I.S.C. personality inventory for each member. Several versions are available for a small fee by searching online. The study will analyze who among you is: D— Driver; I—Influencer; S—Steady; C—Conscientious. Every effective leadership team needs all four personality styles, and each member needs to understand how they interact. You can send each member a link by e-mail to complete the study before the next meeting. It will require less than an hour for each person to complete the inventory. Further analyze your team roles by identifying who has the spiritual gifts of apostle, prophet, evangelist, pastor, and teacher as listed in Ephesians 4.
- Develop a covenant statement presenting what the leadership team can expect from you as leader. Be specific and include punctuality, communication, your leadership style, and anything else crucial to team success. The covenant will be completed at the next meeting.
- A major key to leadership is found in the concept of communication saturation. Constantly communicate the vision and the process until those around you are saturated with it and can clearly express it to others.

Here is an agenda for your second meeting:

- Present what team members can expect from you as the leader. Invite them to add what you can expect from them as team members. Plan to present the final version of this team covenant at the next meeting for everyone to sign.
- As a team, review and revise your mission statement, smart goals, and action plans. This interaction is crucial. Working together to shape the vision gives your leaders ownership for the vision and the process of reaching it. Be open to their ideas and input. God will work through them to continue to shape your vision to his will.
- Discuss the DISC personality inventory results and ask them to identify their spiritual gift as apostle, prophet, evangelist, pastor, or teacher. Ask each member to lead a specific area of responsibility based on their own giftedness and availability. Accept thankfully whatever they

can offer. Their willingness to contribute should increase as they see progress toward the vision.

- Ask them to recruit an apprentice who will serve with them. Dave and Jon Ferguson in their book *Exponential,* describe the process of apprenticeship: Step one = I do, you watch, we talk; Step two = I do, you help, we talk; Step three = You do, I help, we talk; Step Four = You do, I watch, we talk; Step Five = You do, someone else watches.[9] Every leader throughout a missional organization should have an apprentice in order to grow exponentially. Effective leadership development is the key to the future of your vision. Do not skip this step!
- Agree to pray daily at a specific hour for each other and for God's guidance. Schedule the next meeting then adjourn.

Send a reminder for each team member to recruit and invite their apprentice to attend the next meeting. Share resources and thoughts through your blog/contact list.

Here is a suggested agenda for the third meeting of the leadership team:

- Have each team member introduce his or her apprentice.
- Present the final version of the team covenant and ask each member to sign it.
- Review the revised mission statement, smart goals, and action plans as finalized in the previous meeting. Ensure that everyone agrees and is ready to act on them.
- Assemble a list of potential recruits for each action team. Ask each leadership team member to recruit their action team and begin work before the next meeting. Agree to report progress by means of the e-contact list.
- Recommit to pray daily at a specific hour for each other and for God's guidance. Schedule the next meeting and adjourn.

In Nehemiah chapter three, Nehemiah named his leadership team and recounted the action plan each accomplished to complete the re-building of Jerusalem. Continue leading your team to accomplish their assignments. The vision will become reality by reaching your smart goal as your leadership team fulfills their assigned action plans.

9. Ferguson, *Exponential*, 79.

Step six: Respond to opposition and conflict

> But when Sanballat the Horonite, Tobiah the Ammonite official, and Geshem the Arab heard about it, they mocked and ridiculed us. "What is this you are doing?" they asked. "Are you rebelling against the king?" I answered them by saying, "The God of heaven will give us success. We his servants will start rebuilding, but as for you, you have no share in Jerusalem or any claim or historic right to it." Nehemiah 2:19–20, NIV

Every vision will encounter opposition. God's chosen nation spent time in the wilderness between slavery and the Promised Land, and you will, too. The DISC personality inventory mentioned earlier tells us that 40 percent of us are "S" personalities. "S" personalities value steadiness, staying the course, and maintaining the status quo. Charles Arn, in his book, *How to Start a New Service*, identifies five levels of receptivity to change:[10]

- Innovators—Dreamers/Visionaries who embrace the future and are eager to embrace change but may not be accepted as leaders.
- Early Adopters—Those who embrace a good idea on its own merit and are influential in moving it forward.
- Middle Adopters—The majority. They tend to want to maintain the status quo and are influenced most by those opposing change rather than those supporting it.
- Late Adopters—The last to endorse a new idea. Often they will not support any change regardless of merit until after it is adopted by the majority.
- Never Adopters—Tend to be anti-change and will sow discord before, during, and after change is adopted.

Nehemiah experienced confrontation with detractors also. Nehemiah's enemies circulated a rumor that his ambition was to become king. They planted the rumor to discredit him and undermine the mission. His three critics lived in his homeland but were not kindred. Expect there to be some who are not kindred spirits to your mission. Resistance will come; plan for it. I call this "anticipating some failure to reach more success."

Casey Stengel, New York Yankee baseball manager in the 1950s, once said the key to leadership is to keep the five people who hate you away

10. Arn, *How to Start a New Service*, 66–67.

from the four who are undecided. In most organizations facing change, the middle adopters tend to listen to late adopters and never adopters. Your task as a leader is to empower the early adopters to inspire and lead the middle adopters to new ground. An unknown source, tongue-in-cheek, has delineated five stages of innovation:

- Step One—People deny the innovation is required;
- Step Two—People deny the innovation will justify the effort;
- Step Three—People deny the innovation is important;
- Step Four—People deny the innovation is effective;
- Step Five—People accept the innovation, enjoy its benefits, attribute it to someone other than the innovator, and deny the existence of steps one through four.

When experiencing persecution, follow the example of Jesus. Jesus laid down his life for us. Don't allow yourself to be a doormat to your critics, but do lay yourself down as a bridge to grace. We are most like Jesus when we share grace with someone who doesn't deserve it. A servant leader imitating Jesus will absorb pain in his body to the point of brokenness. But our Lord has been there for us. On the other hand, Jesus also reserved some of his most confrontational words for religious critics. The ability to balance both godly grace and careful confrontation grows from brokenness before God. Remain a servant-leader, just as Jesus served us and died for us.

Step seven: Celebrate success

> At the dedication of the wall of Jerusalem, the Levites were sought out from where they lived and were brought to Jerusalem to celebrate joyfully the dedication with songs of thanksgiving and with the music of cymbals, harps and lyres . . . I also assigned two large choirs to give thanks . . . And on that day they offered great sacrifices, rejoicing because God had given them great joy. The sound of rejoicing in Jerusalem could be heard far away. Nehemiah 12:27, 31, 43 (NIV)

You have envisioned the dream, shared it with others, and led them to join you in accomplishing it. It wasn't easy, and bringing it to reality required leading in the face of criticism and challenges. But you led through change into action. Now understand, this is only one small step in a long journey.

Leadership experts remind us that it takes five to seven years to truly change a culture. So dig in and lead for the long haul.

Now God stands ready to show you the next missional step he has for you in the journey. Before you move on to your next mission there are two things that are crucial:

1. Worship, praise, and thanks to God;
2. Reward and recognition of the people.

When we praise God for success, we are recognizing that God gave the vision and all the resources to accomplish it. Because everything in life flows from God and to God, diverting any of the glory for ourselves is foolish. Leave no room for anyone to think you brought the victory. Offer your sacrifice of praise with such totality that there is no mistaking that God is getting all the credit.

Step eight: Build future vision on past vision and present relationships

> But while all this was going on, I was not in Jerusalem, for in the thirty-second year of Artaxerxes king of Babylon I had returned to the king. Some time later I asked his permission and came back to Jerusalem. Here I learned about the evil thing Eliashib had done . . . I rebuked the nobles of Judah and said to them, "What is this wicked thing you are doing—desecrating the Sabbath day? Didn't your forefathers do the same things, so that our God brought this calamity upon us and upon this city? So I purified the priests and the Levites of everything foreign, and assigned them duties, each to his own task. Nehemiah 13:6–7,17–18,30, NIV

Nehemiah's first vision was to re-build the city of Jerusalem. His next vision was to purify the people. While in captivity and immersed in another culture, they had compromised the purity of their Jewish faith. Nehemiah's intent was to restore their allegiance to the one true God—the God of their forefathers who would use them to bring forth the Savior. In some ways, rebuilding the city must have seemed easy compared to changing the attitudes, habits, and daily practices of the people.

As you celebrate the victory of achieving your first vision, remember that the process of transformation is ongoing. The mission effort you have begun is very fragile. It must be nourished and protected in order to take root. Regression can happen before you know it. A single accomplishment will be an empty victory if we return to old patterns of hoarding our giftedness. Being missional requires an ongoing intent, focus, and plan. It will take years for missional thinking to be fully ingrained in an organization that has been self-centered.

The ability to manage change will always depend on the quality of your relationships. I am amused to read in Nehemiah how he resorted to strong-arm tactics of pulling hair out and beating up those who disobeyed the laws of Jewish purification (Nehemiah 13:25). A leader must certainly be willing to discipline those who disobey God's laws. But a leader can never withdraw from the bank account more than he has invested in his people relationally. Nehemiah had said previously: "The earlier governors—those preceding me—placed a heavy burden on the people . . . Their assistants also lorded it over the people. But out of reverence for God I did not act like that" (Neh. 5:15, NIV). We must constantly check our "relational balance statement" to ensure that we are depositing more care, attention, encouragement, and love in our follower's lives than we ask for in return. That is servant-leadership by Christ's example.

As you are nearing realization of this first missional masterpiece, begin to envision your next work. Go to God and ask him to breathe another vision into your brokenness. Go back to your pastor and begin the circle all over again. Keep on dreaming and leading full circle. Never stop until he calls you home or returns to take you there.

Return to the Cross

If you aspire to be a leader of disciples, be cautious! "Sin is crouching at your door; it desires to have you, but you must master it" (Gen. 4:7, NIV) The biggest challenge we face as leaders is the mastery of our private self. What am I when no one is looking?

Alas, and did my Savior bleed and did my Sovereign die?
Would He devote that sacred head for sinners such as I?
Was it for crimes that I had done, he groaned upon the tree?
Amazing pity, grace unknown, and love beyond degree![11]

11. Watts, "Alas, and Did My Savior Bleed," Public Domain.

I shudder to think of the whip on Jesus' back. I do not want to imagine the cat-of-nine-tails bruising and cutting him for me. Yet I persist in my sin, heaping pain on him. Are you too weak to embrace the pain of rejecting secret sin when he took the whip and nails for you? By his stripes we are healed. They are his gift to you. Allow the image of his stripes to overpower private sin. That is your gift to him. Our choice is to either be healed or hold the whip.

Well might the sun in darkness hide, and shut His glories in,
When Christ the mighty Maker died for man, the creature's sin.
But drops of grief can ne'er repay the debt of love I owe;
Here, Lord, I give myself away, 'Tis all that I can do.

Questions for Thought and Discussion

Do you know of people who have rejected change even though change was in their best interest? Do you know of others who have successfully made necessary changes? What were the results?

What are some specific ways you can use powerful questions, storying, and testimonies to appeal to the emotions of those resisting change?

What changes do you need to make in your own attitudes and lifestyle to walk with God in total trust?

How does the story of Nehemiah's mission to re-build the wall correspond to your own mission? What can you learn from his leadership?

What step in the leadership process concerns you most? What step do you feel most confident of your ability to accomplish?

As a personal exercise, fill out the detailed strategy worksheet in Step 5 to develop a preliminary vision statement, smart goals, and action plans.

Commit to meet God every day and pray for the vision he has in mind for you. Write the time and place here.

Time:

Place:

14

A Missional Discipleship Plan

While they were eating, He said, "I assure you: One of you will betray Me."

Deeply distressed, each one began to say to Him, "Surely not I, Lord." . . .

Then Judas, His betrayer, replied, "Surely not I, Rabbi?"

"You have said it," He told him.

Matthew 26:20-22,25-26, HCSB

DISCIPLE OR BETRAYER, THE difference is found in one small word. The disciples called Jesus "Lord," but Judas called him "Rabbi," which means "teacher." Many in the world know information about Jesus. But knowledge alone does not make a disciple. When Jesus is our Lord, he is our master, our spiritual boss, our authority. "To Judas, Jesus was a rabbi he respected, spent time with, and learned from, but Jesus was not lord of his life. Judas never surrendered his will to Jesus. He was informed but never transformed."[1] A disciple's life is the expression of deep love for our Lord and Savior who transforms us daily through his power.

In chapter eight, we studied the transformation process Jesus outlined in the Beatitudes. There we discovered how God transforms believers into disciples. How can we partner with God to develop a plan which will lead worship teams through transformation? How can we provide experiences to grow worship teams into missionaries? Here is a three-step plan

1. Geiger, Kelley, Nation, *Transformational Discipleship*, 19.

to transform your worship team into a missional worship team over the course of the coming months.

Step One: The Missional Life Retreat.

Your first step needs to introduce your worship team to missional thinking. We cannot expect them to grow into deeper discipleship and more active missions until they have developed the missional mindset. The first step to introduce these concepts to your team is to host a missional life retreat. During this retreat, you will rehearse and prepare music for upcoming corporate worship while you are introducing basic missional life concepts.

The best time of year for this retreat to occur is in either early January or just after Labor Day. An alternative could be a few weeks after Easter, but our hectic spring schedules make this alternative the third choice. The retreat could be scheduled on a Saturday morning, Sunday afternoon, or week night. It can be effective if held in your own rehearsal space, though you might want to consider an offsite retreat.

Here is the outline for a missional life retreat:

- Enjoy fellowship time with light snacks, 30 minutes before official start time.
- Warm up and rehearse worship songs for the upcoming Sunday.
- Present videos, testimonies and statistics introducing the decline of Christian affiliation in our country. Then present stories of needs in your community: spiritual darkness, illiteracy, teen pregnancy, crime, illicit drug use, etc. Consider inviting someone from the police or sheriff's department, a school administrator, or a social worker to share local stories of need. Ask your worship team to share a two-minute story of needs and challenges they see in the community with the person on their right. Explain the concept of "going full circle" and how our worship must move us to deeper discipleship and active missions. Lead a time of prayer and sing a song for God to open our eyes to see our world as he sees it.
- Rehearse another song or two for future worship services. Choosing songs to learn and rehearse that reflect our call to missional living will strengthen the impact of the event.
- Ask your team to discuss these questions with the person on their left: Where in the Bible does it say that we will win the world by getting

people into church? What does it say? Teach them the five-fingered-approach-to-handing-someone-the-gospel. Ask them to share with the whole group ideas about how this approach could be applied in your community by your worship team. Have a time of prayer led by those previously recruited to pray on the team's behalf.

- Rehearse one or more upcoming songs for future worship services. Present videos of missional concepts. Some sources for missional videos that can be bought and downloaded are: www.ignitermedia.com; www.worshiphousemedia.com; www.sermonspice.com. (Note: You may use videos from YouTube or Vimeo or other web-sharing sites only if you are live-streaming the video from the Internet, according to current U.S. copyright laws.) Ask for quick first-impression responses to these videos from your worship team.

The retreat should continue in this pattern, alternating rehearsal of upcoming worship songs, with teaching of basic missional concepts from this book and other resources, followed by guided discussion. Be sure to invite your lead pastor to come in and say a closing word of support and encouragement to the team for their vision. Close the retreat with a celebrative ending and commitment to continue to the next step. Announce step two, missional moments, to begin in the next rehearsal. Celebrate this launch of full-circle living in your worship ministry.

Step Two: Missional Moments in Rehearsals.

During weekly rehearsals (preferably not at the end), take five minutes to teach basic concepts of worship, discipleship, and mission from this book and other resources. Share stories by video or webcast conferencing of worship teams that are successfully doing missions in their community. Remember to target emotional impact for real change by using stories, Scripture, testimonies, and videos to illustrate each point. Exercise careful discipline to stay on task and within time constraints. Invite a worship team member to close with prayer for your team to apply the concept taught each session.

There is no particular duration that I can suggest for this step. You, as leader, will have to ascertain when your team is ready to move to the next step. Be extremely sensitive to anyone who seems to be hearing God's call to be a missional leader or leadership team member. During this step, you should begin to personally recruit your mission team that will work with you to plan and produce a mission project in your community. But be careful not to recruit only those who are Innovators, eager to embrace change but not trusted as leaders. You will need Early Adopters who are trusted leaders possessing influence necessary to move your vision toward action plans and lead in that process. Also, during this step, begin to promote participation in the next step, full circle groups.

Step Three: Full Circle Groups

> Jesus went out and saw a tax collector named Levi sitting at the tax office, and He said to him, "Follow Me!" So, leaving everything behind, he got up and began to follow Him. Luke 5:27–28, HCSB

As a third step to introduce your team to missional thinking, I propose full circle groups for worshipers and worship leaders based on the Real Life Ministries model. Our goal is to grow spiritual dynamos who are fully invested in going full circle with God.

Real Life Ministries (RLM) is a non-denominational Evangelical Christian church in Post Falls, Idaho. Planted in 1998, the church has grown to an average weekend attendance of more than 7,000. The unique characteristic of Real Life is a Bible study methodology called storying that grew out of a partnership with Avery Willis. Willis who served as president of an Indonesian seminary, wrote *MasterLife* discipleship plan, served as executive strategist for 5,500 missionaries with the International Mission Board, and ended his career with the International Orality Network.

After several years of discussion with Willis, Real Life decided to introduce the orality method of Bible-storying into their small groups. The experiment was so successful that they trained all their pastors, community pastors, and small group leaders in the method. They found that the storying method:

- Helps people learn the Bible,
- Makes it easier to recruit small group leaders,
- Facilitates real learning,
- Equips members for ministry,
- Empowers parents to disciple their kids,
- Helps small group leaders understand the spiritual needs of those they are discipling,

- Keeps small groups from becoming boring, and
- Encourages transparency and real relationships.[2]

Real Life identifies three major keys to making disciples according to God's plan:

1. An intentional leader,
2. A relational environment, and
3. A reproducible process.[3]

The Real Life Discipleship Training Manual presents the mathematical process of kingdom multiplication:

- One disciple makes three disciple-makers every five years.
- If those three disciple-makers do the same every five years, in ten years there will be almost 180,000 disciple-makers.
- If they continue, in seventy years (less than the average life span) there are potentially fourteen billion disciple-makers. That is twice the number of people currently occupying our planet.[4]

The Real Life storying method has proven successful for growing disciples through the local church, so I have applied it here for worship leaders.

Do you feel God's call to start a full circle group for your worship leaders? First, you need to pray with all your might. Pray that God will lead you to the worship leaders on your team who most need to be brought into this group. Remember that we are "calling out the called," not just pressing people into service. If someone resists being a part of the group, even if you feel strongly that they should join, don't force the issue. Pray that God will call out those he has called and move in their spirits to enlist willingly. Ask God to equip you with the skill to lead a group that will grow mature disciples. And pray for courage to find personal openness and transparency in group relationships yourself. This is a challenge for worship leaders because we are hesitant to be vulnerable to church members. Pray, too, that God will grow each participant to start a full circle group after successfully participating in the original group. Replication of groups at least annually

2. Sells, "Discipleship Revolution," *Mission Frontiers*, page unknown.

3. Putnam, Willis, Guindon, Krause, *Real-Life Discipleship Training Manual: Equipping Disciples Who Make Disciples*, 60.

4. Ibid., 75.

is an important key to making disciples who make disciples. Allowing a single group to meet for a year without replication will invite the group to turn inward. Be sure this plan for replication is clearly understood by all leaders and participants.

Throughout the sessions, it is crucial that your group develop and perform a mission project to your community. The greatest temptation for any discipleship group is self-centeredness. It will be easy to give in to our sinful nature and focus only on our own needs within the group. But full circle groups must develop worshiping disciples on mission. If our intent becomes focused on meeting our own needs, we will have simply recast idolatry in the same old drama with a new script. Find a project together and go on mission. Mission will give your group the context to grow. Remember, Jesus sent his disciples on mission very soon after he called them. Hear his mandate to your group to be on mission from the start as you grow in relational discipleship.

If you decide to lead your worship ministry to establish full circle groups, start personally enlisting spiritually mature group leaders immediately as you begin missional moments in rehearsals. It is very important to recruit these leaders face-to-face rather than by phone or e-mail.

Once your leaders are recruited, immediately saturate the whole worship team with promotion of the full circle groups. This will build on the momentum from the retreat and the weekly teaching in rehearsals. At that time, you can equip your leaders to recruit group members personally, also face-to-face. This will greatly strengthen the relational element of the groups since they will be recruited relationally.

Full circle groups for worship leaders may meet during a weekly Bible teaching hour such as Sunday morning or evening or another night, an extra hour before rehearsal, or for breakfast or lunch meetings. Locations might include church, home, office, school, or a public meeting room. Be creative and think outside the box. Being intentionally cross-generational is a wonderful way to provide mentoring and networking for people in different life-stage and social groups. Do your best to find people from many generations and lifestyles to bring together in your groups to learn from each other.

> And let us consider how we may spur one another on toward love and good deeds. Let us not give up meeting together, as some are in the habit of doing, but let us encourage one another. Hebrews 10:24–25a, NIV

Full circle groups foster relationships while participants engage in discussion, personal transparency, application, and mission action. They also cultivate ongoing transformation and accountability as the group achieves deeper levels of relationship. And, like Jesus with his disciples, they are sent on mission early in the process.

Here is a suggested agenda for leading a full circle group for worship leaders in your church:

1. Set the scene. The group leader must arrive early. Prayer-walk the setting as you enter the building. Whether a home, classroom, or other location, ask God to make his presence known in that place today. Ensure that the setting is private and will not allow for interruptions or loss of confidentiality from those nearby who might overhear conversations. Set up chairs in a circle facing each other and check the room for comfort.

2. Greet the group. Establish a relaxed and friendly atmosphere as the group arrives and allow them just a few minutes to establish their group identity with casual conversation.

3. Teach the Bible story. Start on time. At each group meeting, a different group member will volunteer to be the story-teller. A volunteer for the following week will be enlisted at the end of the session.

- The leader will begin by asking those present to share some experiences they had during the past week as they shared last week's story with others. Ask: "How has God worked through you as his missionary since our last meeting?" After a few minutes of sharing, the leader will call on this week's storyteller to begin today's story.

- The storyteller for this session will begin by saying: "This is the story from God's word." They then re-tell today's Bible story from memory in their own words in an engaging manner that reflects their own personality. They should not add personal comments or explanation and should conclude by saying: "That's the story from God's word."

- The storyteller will ask someone to lead a prayer asking God to reveal his will for each participant in today's group.

- The storyteller directs the group to look at today's Bible story in the Scripture. The storyteller will ask "what" and "why" questions of the group about the story. In this way, they will rebuild the story, checking to see if any element was omitted or accidentally changed.

- Discuss: "Which character in the story do you relate to most? Why?"
- Discuss: "What did you learn from this story that is new to you? What surprised you?"
- Discuss: "What do we learn about God from this story?"
- Discuss: "What do we learn about people from this story?"
- Discuss: "How do you think God wants you to apply what you have learned?"
- Accountability Question: "With whom will you share the story this week?"
- Accountability question: "Where will you be on mission with God before our next meeting?"
- Invite the group to pray aloud for each other to close the group study.
- Enlist a storyteller for the next session.
- Remind the group of total confidentiality of everything shared today. This is crucial and must be honored at all times.
- State the next meeting date/time and then dismiss.

4. Send the group out. End on time. Allow the group to dismiss and depart casually according to the group's personality.

The simplicity of the storying method of Bible study is obvious. This simplicity creates a reproducible process in a relational environment, and this is the key to the method's appeal and accessibility. Using this simple method, you can start a full circle group in your worship ministry and lead it to multiply throughout your church and community every six to twelve months. And further, by adopting a mission project for the duration of your group, you are creating a missional community with a goal of establishing a mission outpost that may become an indigenous church with ongoing cultivation. This necessitates careful planning to pass a project on to other groups as you multiply. Again, the adoption of a group or individual mission project is crucial to the spiritual growth of the group. Without a missional intent, groups will fail to go full circle.

> Jesus spoke all these things to the crowd in parables;
> he did not say anything to them without using a parable.
> Matthew 13:34, NIV

Jesus knew the power of stories to communicate truth. When we think of Jesus, we naturally think of his teaching in parables. Stories conveying truth occur throughout the Bible. Bible stories are actual historic accounts while parables are metaphors that are developed to illustrate a point of truth. Both are wonderful means of conveying truth through storying.

Avery Willis in 2005 noted the changes in America that are opening the door for storying in our own society: "The post-modern culture drives much of the revival of storytelling in the United States . . . Most of today's younger generation and even many of the baby boomers of the 50's, 60's and 70's prefer to learn through spoken and visual means rather than written word. There is also a preference towards relational, non-linear learning . . . The problem before us is that most of our preaching, Bible studies, evangelism and discipleship are reader-oriented and very linear-sequential. So how do we change? That is the question of the hour. We must do something before this wave engulfs us and before we lose a whole generation for the cause of Christ."[5]

Here is a list of Bible stories and Scripture references for a curriculum to lead your group through the missional life circle. These Bible stories focus first on worship, then discipleship, and finally missions for worship leaders. The stories are listed in chronological order as they occur in Scripture. But you may use them in the order that best fits your full circle group. There are eighteen stories listed, six each under the headings of worship-discipleship-mission.

Worship

- Numbers 8:5–26: Calling and commissioning the Levites, worship leaders in the Tabernacle.
- 1 Chronicles 29:1–20: David called the nation of Israel to build the temple.
- Isaiah 6:1-8: God revealed himself to Isaiah in the temple.
- Matthew 28:16–20: Jesus' followers worshiped him and he gave them the Great Commission.
- Acts 16:16–40: Paul and Silas worshiped in prison; earthquake freed them for mission.
- Revelation 4:1–11: Worship in heaven around God's throne.

5. Willis, "Storying Going Mainstream."

Discipleship

- Daniel 3: The golden image and the fiery furnace.
- Daniel 6: Daniel in the lion's den.
- Matthew 4:18–22: Jesus calling the first disciples.
- Luke 4:1–13: Satan tempted Jesus.
- Mark 10:17–31: The rich young man.
- John 13:1-30: The greatest commandment.

Mission

- Jonah 1:1 to 3:5: God called Jonah to missions.
- Matthew 9: 9–23: Jesus ate with sinners, taught about wineskins, and healed many.
- Matthew 18:1–6: Who is the greatest?
- Luke 10:25–37: The parable of the good Samaritan.
- Acts 15: 1–12: The Jerusalem Council.
- Acts 17:16–34: Paul preached in Athens.

> And he will go on before the Lord, in the spirit and power of Elijah, to turn the hearts of the fathers to their children and the disobedient to the wisdom of the righteous—to make ready a people prepared for the Lord. Luke 1:17, NIV

In chapter six, I quoted from the book *The Emotionally Healthy Church* in delineating the four stages of spiritual growth: emotional infant, emotional child, emotional adolescent, and emotional adult. Interestingly, RLM uses similar classifications to indicate the level of spiritual growth in its RLM group members: Spiritually Dead, Spiritual Infants, Spiritual Children, Spiritual Young Adults, and Spiritual Parents. RLM's reproducible process attempts to share the gospel with the spiritually dead, share life and basic teaching with spiritual infants, connect spiritual children in relationships within God's family, help spiritual young adults mature through ministry, and release spiritual parents to disciple others.

Educators often speak of "learning outcomes," which are markers of successful learning throughout an educational process. Jeff Iorg, president of Golden Gate Theological Seminary, outlined three learning outcomes for disciples: "No matter what we claim . . . education is revealed in what graduates can *do. (Italics his)* The outcomes reveal what was really learned . . . Studying the church at Antioch from this perspective reveals what was taught by Barnabas and Paul."[6]

The account of the Antioch church is found in Acts 11:19–30 and 13:1–3. The writer of Acts wrote that followers of Jesus were first called Christians in Antioch (11:26). Iorg reminded us that though this church was only a year or two old at the time of the writing of Acts, it is regarded as one of the most influential churches in the New Testament. What are the learning outcomes exhibited in their behavior that show spiritual maturity? First, in worship, they knew how to allow God's Spirit to create a worship vortex among them. According to Acts 13:2–3 (HCSB): "As they were ministering to the Lord and fasting, the Holy Spirit said, 'Set apart for me Barnabas and Saul for the work I have called them to.' Then after they had fasted, prayed, and laid hands on them, they sent them off."

Second, in discipleship, they knew how to live sacrificially. According to Acts 11:29 (HCSB): "So each of the disciples, according to his ability, determined to send relief to the brothers who lived in Judea." And third, they knew how to go on mission, both in their community and to other people groups. According to Acts 11:24 (HCSB): "Large numbers of people were added to the Lord" as the church was on mission to its community.

Do these learning outcomes of the Antioch church sound familiar? They are the circle of missional living: worship-discipleship-mission. The fact that they reflected these outcomes proves that Paul and Barnabas taught an intentional process of transformational discipleship. Paul and Barnabas were growing worshiping disciples on mission in Antioch.

Like Paul and Barnabas, a worship leader interested in leading a full circle group should have grown to the stage of spiritual parent. Make no mistake, individuals' spiritual maturity is not revealed by their age, how long they have been a Christian, or even how many years they have attended church. Spiritual maturity, as stated in chapter eight, is best gauged by our transformation in Christ as evidenced by the fruit of the Spirit. Don't be fooled by other more obvious but misleading factors. Does this mean that a person who is a spiritual young adult or spiritual child is not capable of assuming the role of disciple-maker? Let's be honest, that scenario is

6. Iorg, "Learning Outcomes and Discipleship: A Sermon on the Church at Antioch," *SBC Life*, 16.

no better than a teenager or child becoming the foster parent of a toddler. Yet we see this situation all the time in the institutional church. For some strange reason, church members think it is somehow unspiritual to evaluate spiritual growth. So we tend to fill any leadership need with whoever is willing to serve. As a result we end up with spiritually and emotionally immature people in positions of leadership. Why are we so surprised when a spiritual young adult or child gets mad at a spiritual infant and abandons them on the church doorstep?

Avery Willis understood the immaturity prevalent in our churches. The leukemia with which he was diagnosed near Christmas 2009 gave him new insight into a disease that plagues too many churches today. He wrote, "What happens in leukemia is an abnormal development of the DNA in the body, so that the body produces large numbers of immature cells that do not fulfill their design function. I think that is almost a direct parallel to the church today."[7] Willis died in 2010.

In chapter three, I shared a comparison chart between the early church and the institutional church. I sincerely believe that full circle groups will help our churches reclaim the focus and format of the New Testament church. Furthermore, I believe that our worship ministries have the potential to model this method for our churches. Go and do!

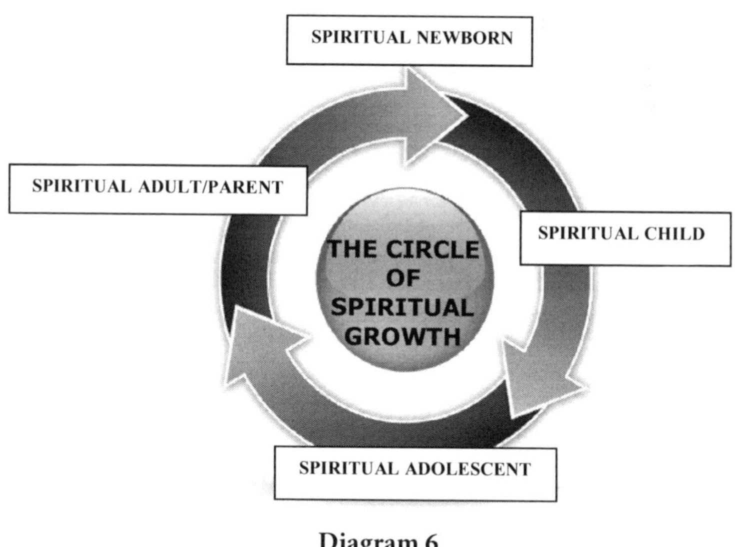

Diagram 6

7. Sells, "Discipleship Revolution," *Mission Frontiers*, page unknown.

Return to the Cross

He was a soldier. He left home to join the army as a young man. He lied about his age. But he was bigger and stronger than his friends. His size helped him get accepted and rise through the ranks. One hundred infantrymen reported to him. But of all the places he had served, why was he stuck now in a Middle Eastern territory trying to keep peace between the Israelis and all their adversaries? It was a never-ending challenge to stay in the good graces of governing bodies arguing over territorial control. But for him it was just another day at the office. He "knew the ropes" and was good at following orders.

Am I a soldier of the cross, A foll'wer of the Lamb?
And shall I fear to own His cause, Or blush to speak His name?
Must I be carried to the skies On flow'ry beds of ease,
While others fought to win the prize,
And sailed through bloody seas?[8]

The day began like any other for this soldier. But it was to be a day he would never forget. Today he was to direct the execution of a prisoner. He drew this duty from time to time, and he found it best to steel his heart and mind against the reality of what he was commanded to do. He knew how to kill a man quickly and was trained to do so. But that was never the plan when dealing with an enemy of the state in this barbaric part of the world. His superiors preferred the execution to be a gruesome example to those who might be contemplating the same course of action. But he was simply following commands.

Are there no foes for me to face? Must I not stem the flood?
Is this vile world a friend to grace, To help me on to God?
Sure I must fight if I would reign; Increase my courage, Lord!
I'll bear the toil, endure the pain,
Supported by Thy Word.

> When they arrived at the place called The Skull, they crucified Him there. The soldiers also mocked Him. It was now about noon, and darkness came over the whole land until three, because the sun's light failed. And Jesus called out with a loud voice, 'Father, into Your hands I entrust My spirit.' Saying this, He breathed His last. When the centurion saw what happened, he began to glorify God, saying, 'This man really was righteous!' All the crowds that had gathered for this spectacle,

8. Watts, "Am I a Soldier of the Cross," Public Domain.

when they saw what had taken place, went home, striking their chests. Luke 23:33a,36a,44–45a,46–48, HCSB

Suddenly, the curtain of the sanctuary was split in two from top to bottom; the earth quaked and the rocks were split. The tombs were also opened and many bodies of the saints who had gone to their rest were raised. When the centurion and those with him, who were guarding Jesus, saw the earthquake and the things that had happened, they were terrified and said, 'This man really was God's Son!" Matthew 27:51–52, 54, HCSB

Questions for Thought and Discussion

What intrigues you about RLM's partnership with Avery Willis to develop a discipleship training process? What is your reaction to Willis' quote about the correlation between his leukemia and the church today?

Review the RLM mathematical process of kingdom multiplication. What one emotion do you experience most when you read this formula for discipling the world?

To what level of spiritual maturity have you progressed in your own life: spiritually unborn, spiritual infant, spiritual child, spiritual young adult, spiritual parent?

What is the value to your worship ministry of leading a missional life retreat and presenting mission moments?

How can you lead those in your sphere of influence to begin a full circle group? Who might God be calling to join this group? Where and when might your group meet?

Are you equipped spiritually and possess the leadership skills to lead a group? If not, who with those qualifications could be recruited to lead? List the strengths of the storying method for growing disciples.

Could you commit to this method and the plan I have outlined for full circle groups? If so, set a target date and write a process you will follow to start a group. Write it at the bottom of this page, underline it and sign it.

15

Strategies for Going

> After consulting the people, Jehoshaphat appointed men to sing to the Lord and to praise him for the splendor of his holiness as they went out at the head of the army, saying: "Give thanks to the Lord, for his love endures forever."
> 2 Chronicles 20:21, NIV

JEHOSHAPHAT PREPARED TO LEAD the army of Judah into battle against the foes gathered at Tekoa. The visible odds against God's people were overwhelming as the armies from three countries had assembled against them. The king first led his people in this well-known prayer, "For we are powerless before this vast multitude that comes to fight against us. We do not know what to do (Lord), but we look to You." (2 Chron. 20:12, HCSB) Then, in faith, Jehoshaphat put the musicians out front to lead the army into battle, worshiping as they moved out to meet the enemy. A great victory was won that day as the enemies of God's people turned against each other in the heat of battle. What an inspiring example this story is for us as worship leaders.

I am totally convinced that your worship ministry can lead your church into revitalization through discipling your team and taking them on mission. If your church is mired in institutionalism, stuck on the wrong track, being held hostage in your building, you can make the difference. Get out of your comfort zone and go full circle to lead your people into worship, discipleship, and mission.

Steve Cloud, of Vision Ventures Inc, reminds us regularly in leadership classes that releasing dreams and building memories don't come while watching television in the recliner or reading blogs in your office.[1]

Finding the sweet spot of life and leadership awaits us outside our comfort zone as we join God's mission. We know this is what God has called us to do. We know that God's ultimate blessing comes when we are moving with him into the world. We know that God has commissioned us to bring our worship team and even our church with us on this journey into missions. So let's go.

> Then Paul stood up in the middle of the Areopagus and said: "Men of Athens! I see that you are very religious in every respect. For as I was passing through and observing the objects of your worship, I even found an altar on which was inscribed: to an unknown god. Therefore, what you worship in ignorance, this I proclaim to you. Acts 17:22–23, HCSB

Paul carefully analyzed the cultural context wherever he went. Here we see him speaking in Athens at the Areopagus, also known as Mars Hill. A council of philosophers met there daily in the open air on the hill. Paul addressed those gathered to discuss and share philosophical ideas. In presenting the gospel to these authorities of secular thought, Paul built a bridge into the culture by referring to an altar placed there in honor of an unknown God. He spoke from their cultural context by quoting two popular Greek philosophers, Cretan philosopher Epimenides and Cilician Stoic philosopher Aratus, in verse 28. Paul had obviously done his homework and carefully analyzed his context.

Here are a few homework questions that you, as a missional artisan, must ask to analyze the cultural context of your own community:

1. What people groups can be found in my community?
2. What are the socio-economic statistics of my community?
3. How many and what kinds of schools are in my community?
4. What kinds of businesses are found here?
5. How many people live here, and what are their ethnicities?
6. What is the crime rate in my community, and where are the hot spots for crime?
7. What is the vision of our local government?

1. Cloud, "Leader's Edge" seminar, South Carolina Baptist Convention, 2010–12.

8. What are the prevalent values in my community, and what entities teach those values?
9. What are the spiritual beliefs found in my community, and what churches are located there?
10. What is our past history, and what demographics will determine our future?
11. What do residents love about my community, and what do they despise?
12. What is the media saying about our community?
13. Who is hurting, and who is succeeding here?

An effective missionary analyzes the cultural context by asking good questions. Poll those who are in daily contact with a wide spectrum of the community: hair stylists, service technicians such as plumbers and cable TV installers working in homes and meeting people, real estate agents, school principals, etc. These individuals are constantly checking the pulse of your community and reading its culture. Enlist them for their helpful insight.

Current data specific to any ZIP code can be accessed on the website for the Intercultural Institute for Contextual Ministry at www.missionalcorps.org. After you have become a registered user on this website, you will find a wealth of statistical information to discern the cultural context of your community and your targeted people groups. This is an amazing tool for worshipers on mission. Access it, get familiar with it, and use it regularly.

Gather all the information and statistics in one written report and use them to develop a strategy to meet people at their point of need on a regular basis in your community to develop relationships that lead to witnessing opportunities. Set up a mission bulletin board where your mission team can view and track your efforts to reach a target group. Print out labels for targeted people groups, their location, and your regular ongoing mission activities among them. Affix the labels to magnetic strips and mount them on a magnetic board. Track individuals by name in those mission settings who are persons of peace, those growing in gospel understanding, and those who have become Christ-followers. Develop SMART goals and action plans to involve them in the mission and grow them as disciples and leaders.

> And pray for us, too, that God may open a door for our message, so that we may proclaim the mystery of Christ.
> Colossians 4:3, NIV

It's time to put an end to quick-hit presentations once a year at the mall or park and calling it missions. Music mission efforts do not necessarily have to include musical performance. When we make it our purpose to meet people at their point of need to build witnessing relationships, we are mirroring the heart of the gospel. This interaction gets people asking questions and wondering what our motives are. Then we are ready to share a witness to Christ's love. There is no expectation that someone will present a devotional, that a public prayer will be offered, or that a worship song will be sung. There is, however, a basic trust that the Holy Spirit will work as we show them the heart of Jesus. It takes personal long-term investment in those to whom God leads you. Be patient. And, of course, if the needs in your community are at the most basic level of food, shelter, medical care, etc., you must start by meeting those needs first.

Here is a menu of missional ideas through which your worship ministry can "get out of the church box" and incarnate the gospel to your own community. These are all designed as opportunities for the five-fingered-approach-to-handing-someone-the-gospel:

- Adopt a school music program: Provide volunteers to help with concerts. Lend them risers, portable sound systems, spotlights, etc. Gather used instruments to donate to band or orchestra members who can't afford them. Offer your church bus and a driver for day trips. Provide private music tutoring or classes in music reading, music history, musical terms, etc.
- Adopt a community theater or concert hall: Provide volunteers (ushers, set builders and painters, stage hands, etc). Take dinner to the theater for the cast and crew at late-night final rehearsals.
- Provide chaplains for school music programs: Athletic teams have chaplains, so why not offer spiritually mature volunteers as band or chorus chaplains in your local schools?
- Present mission music schools: Take your children's or youth music program to the community, and present a weekly music instruction/choir/creative movement/puppet team in a community setting such as a city park, apartment or mobile home community, suburban subdivision, inner city recreation center, etc.
- Do music missions in resort areas: Head to the lake, beach, or mountains and present music activities, storying groups, or recreation for

children, youth, or families in resort areas, parks, recreational areas, campgrounds, etc.

- Reach out to college campuses: Opportunities are virtually unlimited to provide weekly missions to secular college campuses with appropriate permission. Be creative to discover ways to serve students in adopt-a-student programs, helping Christian campus ministry organizations, providing transportation or part-time jobs and other ways you can discover to meet needs.
- Invite people to get involved in a cause: Organize a community walk-a-thon, clean-up day, or service day to homebound residents and then invite the whole community to participate. Make it a monthly event, and build relationships as you work shoulder-to-shoulder with your neighbors.
- Plan neighborhood movie musical nights: Enlist worship team members to show movies of classic family-friendly Broadway musicals in their backyards with friends to cultivate witnessing opportunities. Provide a projector, screen, and portable sound system. (Note: According to Title 17 of the U.S. Copyright Code, no additional license is required to privately view a movie or other copyrighted work with a few friends and family at your home. However, restaurants, private clubs, prisons, lodges, factories, summer camps, public libraries, daycare facilities, parks departments, non-profits, churches, and non-classroom use at schools and universities require a performance license regardless of whether an admission fee is charged.)
- Join your local arts council: Encourage worship team members to get involved in your local arts council or community arts festival committees to build witnessing relationships with artists. Serve on organizational boards of community orchestras and choirs, and offer to host their concerts in your church facility.
- Present a series of block parties: Secure a location in a city park, a subdivision clubhouse, a shopping center parking lot, an apartment or mobile home community, etc. Rent inflatables for children, and give away hotdogs and drinks. Provide carnival games. Set up a stage area with portable sound and have your worship groups sing throughout the event. Give away balloons and promotional items with John 3:16 imprinted. Equip your members to intentionally build witnessing relationships during the event. Provide response cards to gather

information on prospects for follow-up. Identify those who would attend an ongoing home Bible study group near the site of the block party and invite them.

- Enlist your worship team to host Christmas gatherings: Plan a Christmas party where your neighbors can hear and experience the love of Jesus Christ. See http://christmasgatherings.com for information.
- Place mission ministry tables in public places: Provide free snacks and bottled water at arts festivals, foot races, bicycle races, walk-a-thons, or even in hospital waiting rooms or bus stations, walking trails, college back-to-school days, etc. Provide a solo musician to minister through music. Always ask for contact information to find the person of peace who can open the door to ongoing missions in the area.
- Form an acts of kindness team to local artists: Take doughnuts, a newspaper, and coffee (or meet other needs) to your local arts galleries on a regular basis to establish a caring relationship with artists and gallery owners.
- Start a weekly coffeehouse discussion group about spirituality in the arts: Use a web-based service to develop a survey about spirituality in the arts or other issues and distribute invitations to artists to register their input online. Invite local artists who respond to the survey to come together and discuss spiritual influences in their artwork in a weekly coffeehouse setting.
- Place worship artists in local venues on a weekly schedule: Contract with local businesses to provide musicians and artists in local settings (coffee shops, open mic nights, bookstores, galleries, flea markets, etc). Have them present primarily secular works with a spiritual theme. Provide others who are adept at initiating conversation to engage those in the audience.
- Go to jail and prison: Schedule regular visits to a local jail or prison to serve, lead worship, and build relationships.
- Volunteer in homeless shelters and soup kitchens: Intentionally seek to build relationships with those you meet as you serve them.
- Go to drug and alcohol rehabilitation centers and halfway houses: Serve clients and build relationships. Begin conversations that might lead to witnessing opportunities.

- Adopt an assisted living village or retirement center: Provide worship services on Sundays for residents and their families and help residents with other needs each week.
- Get to know your neighbors: Every member of your worship team should actively befriend and serve their neighbors. Invite neighbors over for a cook-out or coffee on the back porch.
- Adopt a ball field: Hand out bottled water and be a missionary in the stands at your local ballpark, sports fields, or basketball courts.
- Pray for restaurant wait staff: As your waiter/waitress brings your order to your table, tell them that you are going to pray a blessing. Ask them if you can pray for them, too. If you discover needs in their lives, use it as an opportunity to share hope in Christ.
- Join a community chorus or barbershop singing group: Join a group and build witnessing relationships.
- Become a Christian street musician/artist: Take your art and hit the streets; be sure to get a street performance license from your city government office if required.
- Become an online missionary: Develop relationships online through social media and chat rooms and use it for witnessing opportunities. Post Bible verses and personal testimonies of God at work in your life, but be real and avoid clichés. See www.namb.net/erc for information on the Evangelism Response Center and share Jesus by phone or web contact.
- Host an arts night in your home: Invite neighbors to share a poem, a song, or artwork; tell a story; or present a skit just for the fun of it. You may be able to share your testimony for Christ in your own presentation, but keep it light.

These ideas are just a few of the possibilities available right in your own community. Pray that God will open your eyes to see the opportunities all around you. Then remember, quick hit methods do not work. Instead, establish mission outposts by meeting people at their point of need on a regular basis in your community to build relationships that lead to witnessing opportunities. Throughout this process, discover persons of peace, begin Bible-storying groups in their homes, apprentice indigenous leaders, and lead those groups to grow into indigenous house churches.

> This is what is written: the Messiah would suffer and rise from the dead the third day, and repentance for forgiveness of sins would be proclaimed in His name to all the nations, beginning at Jerusalem. You are witnesses of these things.
> Luke 24:46–48, HCSB

If we are to effectively witness for Christ and embody the gospel, there are a few common-sense considerations we must observe on the mission field. You might think that these are "no-brainers," but we cannot assume that people know what is appropriate in a mission setting. We must train our worship teams in the basics of acceptable missionary behavior.

- Be sure to secure liability insurance coverage for each event. Perform background checks on anyone in your organization who comes in contact with minors at mission sites. This is imperative for the integrity of our witness.
- Prayer-walk the missions area before and after every mission effort, and never stop praying the whole time you are there.
- Dress toward the fashion of your target group. But be authentic and real. As a middle-age "white guy," I would look foolish ministering in an urban setting dressed like a hip-hop artist. But wearing business clothes in that setting is just as foolish.
- Focus on others and be outgoing. So many times I have seen groups of Christians huddled together talking and laughing among themselves on the mission field, oblivious to those God has brought to them.
- Don't mention your church name or denomination first; that may come later. When someone asks "What are you doing here?" teach your mission team to respond in a number of ways that are non-threatening: "I'm here because I care and want to be actively involved in solutions," "I'm here to show that God is making a difference in my life," "We discovered there was a need here and felt God calling us to help meet that need," "My relationship with God has impacted my life so much that I want to express it somehow. How do you express yourself?" Find a personal response that introduces your story and tests the other person's heart to see if that person will give you permission to share more.
- Be clean, so that your smell is neutral: no bad breath, body odor, heavy cologne, etc.

- Remove sunglasses, even in a bright outdoor setting. Sunglasses prevent eye contact.
- Never be alone with a person of the opposite sex or a minor! This is extremely important in maintaining integrity and avoiding false charges. Do not make this mistake. Stay in sight of the group at all times.
- Be conversational and relational. Don't get so mechanical that it sounds like a sales pitch. Use everyday language and avoid religious jargon. Don't be long-winded.
- Avoid extreme behaviors: getting angry, being pushy, arguing, ridiculing anyone (present or not present). Belligerence, loud talking, and laughing make others uncomfortable. Be quietly confident but not brash.
- Simply lead individuals into conversations about themselves and then ask leading questions about their spirituality. Emphasize that God wants a relationship with them and has made it available through Jesus' death and resurrection. Keep focusing on this gospel message!
- Have key Bible verses so well-learned that you can share God's Word from your heart in the most natural way. But, you don't have to know the answer to every question. It is okay to say, "Yeah, I'm not sure about that. I'm praying for God to show me that answer, too."
- Never ever discuss politics (and I do mean never ever).
- Don't play the role of wealthy provider. It is okay to graciously say No when asked for money.
- Have a plan to maintain the flow of conversation. Many times a witnessing conversation will ebb and flow back and forth toward then away from the main issue. Plan ways to gently bring the conversation back to the main point of God's love.
- Don't belabor the point. If they are not ready to accept Christ as personal Savior, return to friendly conversation and see if you can establish contact for ongoing conversations by e-mail or other written means.[2]

Again, it is our responsibility as leaders to train our people in these appropriate behaviors for missionaries. Don't leave it up to them just to read the guidelines. Plan training sessions and role play effective and ineffective methodology.

2. Rankin and Tadlock, *Basic Training*, 107.

No list could ever contain all the life moments in which you can start conversations that lead to witnessing opportunities. We must be open to the Holy Spirit when he guides to talk with individuals. And most of all, we must be ready with an array of conversational strategies to be missional in any moment. In his book, *Live Like a Missionary: Giving Your Life for What Matters Most*, Jeff Iorg wrote: "When you are deployed with the gospel, you remind yourself before you get out of the car, I am about to enter my missions field. I must be at my best. I must engage people fully. I have a purpose for being here—making friends, showing the love of Jesus, and sharing the gospel (or some part of the gospel). A missional Christian connects with people and prioritizes building relationships with unbelievers—not just being in their general vicinity and hoping for the best."[3]

A clear witness of Christ must be our intentional goal in all we do. Witnessing can happen naturally when you are on mission and sharing the gospel in a way that fits who God made you as an individual. Our postmodern society does not respond as well today to the point-by-point witnessing methods popular in the past. So develop your own personal way of sharing that fits who you are. Simply saying "Tell me your story" or "Tell me about your life" is a good way to get someone to talk about his or her life. Then ask, "May I share my story with you?" Have your personal testimony/salvation story ready to tell quickly and concisely without religious clichés. Share how you came to Christ and what God is doing in your life daily. Continue by reminding the listener that God invites all people to come into relationship with him through Christ's death to pay the debt of our sin. Share how Christ's resurrection proves he has overcome death for all time and opened the door for a relationship that will last forever.

Draw the conversation to a commitment by asking if the person feels God's leading to open his or her life to him. If so, explain that, to enter into the relationship with our heavenly Father, he asks us to surrender our life and heart to him as Lord. If the person responds positively, lead in a prayer that will TAP into God—Thanking/Asking/Promising:

- Thanking God for loving me enough to send Jesus to die for my sin.
- Asking forgiveness for sin that separates me from God.
- Promising to obey and trust God daily for the rest of my life as I live in his Holy Spirit.

3. Iorg, *Live Like a Missionary: Giving Your Life for What Matters Most*, 97–98.

Depending on the situation, it may be best to state that the person can pray this prayer later, in private. If you do this, be sure to ask for the individual's phone number or contact information to follow-up the next day. If someone you have been leading to Christ comes to this point, please do not lose contact. You are that person's rescue society, so be sure to follow-through.

During your follow-up, lead the new Christian to commit to tell friends and family about the salvation decision as soon as possible. Offer to disciple the person yourself on a weekly basis. Invite the individual to your full circle group or other discipleship group. Help the new Christian plug into a local church and become involved in missions. Go full circle with this person until he or she becomes a worshiping disciple on mission. The process is so simple. Go do it!

Return to the Cross

Redeemed, how I love to proclaim it!
Redeemed by the blood of the Lamb;
Redeemed thro' his infinite mercy, His child, and forever I am.
Redeemed, and so happy in Jesus,
No language my rapture can tell;
I know that the light of His presence
With me doth continually dwell.
Redeemed, Redeemed, Redeemed by the blood of the Lamb;
Redeemed, redeemed, His child, and forever I am.[4]

God's great mission in the world is to redeem people. At the cross of Christ, I personally was redeemed by the blood of the Lamb. There my heavenly Father claimed me forever as his child. Redemption is offered to you at the cross, too. The continual light of his presence is the object of our worship. We are his children forever. Redeemed! Now we join God in his mission of redemption for others.

I think of my blessed Redeemer, I think of Him all the day long;
I sing, for I cannot be silent; His love is the theme of my song.
I know I shall see in His beauty The King in whose law I delight;
Who lovingly guardeth my footsteps
And giveth me songs in the night.
Redeemed, Redeemed, Redeemed by the blood of the Lamb;
Redeemed, redeemed, His child, and forever I am.

4. Crosby, Fanny, "Redeemed, How I Love to Proclaim It," Public Domain.

Fanny Crosby, who wrote this song, lived from 1820 to 1915. Though blinded as an infant, she wrote 8,000 hymns with more than 100 million of her songs in print. Ira Sankey, song leader for the Dwight Moody evangelistic crusades, attributed the success of their efforts largely to Crosby's songs. She knew personally every U.S. president during her adult life. Crosby often said that she lamented not being born blind, so that the first face she would ever see would be that of her Redeemer. But despite being a household name by 1900, Crosby was most committed to Christian rescue missions and well-known for generous donations and speaking on their behalf. At the end of her life, she made it clear to numerous interviewers that she wished to be remembered most as a city rescue mission worker. Crosby lived her life redeemed—going full circle in worship, discipleship, and missions.

Questions for Thought and Discussion

Look back at the cultural context questions listed in this chapter. Answer those questions about your own community.

Who will you approach to help you gain more insight into your community's cultural context? What other resources will you research? To whom will you submit a written report of your findings?

Commit to pray every day, at the specific time committed earlier, for God to point you in the direction where he is calling you to join him on mission in your community. List here others you will invite to pray with you.

From the menu of missional ideas listed in this chapter, choose three opportunities (or develop your own ideas) where your worship ministry can go on mission in the coming months.

What will be your first step in moving toward talking to your pastor and developing a team to accomplish a mission project in your community? Write the target date here by which you plan to complete this first step.

16

A Vision that Goes Full Circle

Joshua told the people, "Consecrate yourselves, for tomorrow the Lord will do amazing things among you." Joshua 3:5, NIV

It's a recurring dream of mine—a vision, really. After many years, we have moved out from the Church Train. In the past, we spent lots of time maintaining our Church Train, meticulously polishing our club car, and planning activities for those on the train. Now we've parked the train. The train is still our base of operations, but we've moved out on mission as individuals and small groups.

Sure, we were headed somewhere on our Church Train, but we were headed for a cliff on the track we were on. At first, we ignored the warnings. To be honest, we just didn't believe it could be true. But it soon became obvious we were headed for a rapid decline and a big crash. So we studied how to build an alternate track. But the cost of a new track and the time required to build it was out of reach. We began to question the need for a track. After all, that track was taking us in only one direction. And despite our constant efforts to attract others to join us on the train, very few wanted to board our train. Then the question came. Where does the Bible say we will win the world primarily by inviting people to board our train? So we parked the train and moved out into our communities. We moved out as mission teams and began to serve people through regular, weekly mission projects in our communities and beyond.

We were exhausted from the worship wars, but those first few months felt like another war of a different kind. We were entering the battle in the world between good and evil. So we gather back at the train weekly to worship God in spirit and truth, lifting Jesus above all, as we encourage and equip each other for the mission. The unity that we feel in those gatherings is amazing, and the equipping we receive there is vital to our daily life as God's missionaries. We fall more deeply in love with him every week, expressing our worship in the heart languages of the people meeting there. Our ultimate goal in life is to grow disciples of Jesus who go make disciples of others. Church life used to be focused on growing people in relationship with the Church Train. Now it's all about growing us into relationship with God and sending us out to join him in his mission. We are truly becoming worshiping disciples on mission.

In our communities, we are meeting people at their point of need. Both individually and in small groups, we build relationships with those we serve. Some of them are very open to us and introduce us to their families and friends. We have been sharing the gospel with them naturally while we serve them. Of course, some of them rejected us completely and will have nothing to do with us now. And several of those from our Church Train went and found another train to get back on the old track. Yet others in our communities have come to know Jesus as Savior and Lord. These have opened their homes to Bible storying groups. They are growing to understand how much God loves them and wants a relationship with them. And some have begun to join us on mission projects. We pray that these home groups may become indigenous churches in our community over the coming months and years.

The changes have come slowly, and we've had to be patient. This new missional mindset has been such a change from the old mindset of maintaining the church club car that we sometimes wish for the simplicity of the past. We must consistently guard against the temptation to return to the old habits of self-focused worship and ministry. So many challenges remain, but those challenges grow from being on mission with God, rather than from arguments on the train about our own comfort and preferences. We pray that God will increase our vision for his mission as we continue to move out.

So, let me ask, what is the status of your train? Do you sense that a crash is just ahead? Do you want to be God's agent of change? You are already an answer to our prayer that God will awaken individuals on the many trains blindly heading toward a meaningless collapse. First and foremost, trust God while you work with persistence and patience. It takes time to stop a train. Only God can change a heart. You can't change the hearts of the folks on your train. Pray and work—work and pray. Go on mission and take some friends with you while you watch for God to change hearts around you. Go make some new friends in your neighborhood and meet their needs. Cultivate relationships and find those people of peace. They don't know it, but they are waiting on you to find them for God.

Our deepest desire is to fulfill his mandate to be worshiping disciples on mission with him. It's a dream, a vision really. And we pray that God will keep us going full circle.

Bibliography

Books

Arn, Charles. *How to Start a New Service.* Grand Rapids: Baker Books, 1998.

Blackaby, Henry, and Richard Blackaby. *Spiritual Leadership: Moving People on to God's Agenda.* Nashville: B & H Publishing Group, 2011.

Breen, Mike, and Alex Absalom, *Launching Missional Communities: A Field Guide.* Myrtle Beach, S.C.: Sheriar Press, 2010.

Chambers, Oswald. *My Utmost for His Highest.* Grand Rapids, Mich.: Discovery House Publishers, 1992.

Cornwall, Judson. *Worship as Jesus Taught It.* Tulsa, Ok.: Victory House Publishers, 1987.

Drucker, Peter. *The Essential Drucker: The Best of Sixty Years of Peter Drucker's Essential Writings on Management.* New York: Harper Collins Publishers. 2008.

Ferguson, Dave, and Jon Ferguson. *Exponential.* Grand Rapids: Zondervan, 2010.

Finney, John. *Recovering the Past: Celtic and Roman Mission.* London: Darton, Longman & Todd, 1996.

Geiger, Eric, et al. *Transformational Discipleship.* Nashville: B & H Books, 2012.

Hawkins, Greg, and Cally Parkinson. *Reveal: Where are You?* South Barrington, Ill.: Willow Creek Association, 2008.

Iorg, Jeff. *Live Like a Missionary: Giving Your Life for What Matters Most.* Birmingham: New Hope Publishing, 2011.

Kauflin, Bob. *Worship Matters: Leading Others to Encounter the Greatness of God.* Wheaton, Ill.: Crossway Books, 2008.

MacArthur, John. *The Jesus You Can't Ignore.* Nashville: Thomas Nelson, 2009.

Mayfield, Bob. *Missional Pivot Points,* 22. Oklahoma City: Baptist General Convention of Oklahoma, 2009.

McNeal, Reggie. *Missional Communities: The Rise of the Post-Congregational Church.* San Francisco: Jossey-Bass, 2011.

Miller, Donald. *Blue Like Jazz.* Nashville: Thomas Nelson, 2003.

Moore, Beth. *Daniel: Lives of Integrity, Words of Prophecy.* Nashville: LifeWay Press, 2006.

Moore, Dwayne. *Pure Praise.* Loveland Colo.: Group Publishing, 2008.

Piper, John. *Let the Nations Be Glad.* Grand Rapids: Baker Books, 1993.

Price, Milburn, and Gary Furr. *Dialogue of Worship: Creating Space for Revelation and Response.* Macon, Ga.: Smith & Helwys Publishing Inc., 1998.

Putnam, Jim, et al. *Real-Life Discipleship Training Manual: Equipping Disciples Who Make Disciples.* Colorado Springs: NavPress, 2010.

Rankin, Jerry and Phyllis Tadlock. *Basic Training for Mission Teams.* Richmond: International Mission Board, 2006.

Sayers, Dorothy. *Christian Letters to a Post Christian World.* Grand Rapids: William B. Eerdmans Publishing Co, 1969.

Scazzero, Pete, and Warren Bird. *The Emotionally Healthy Church.* Grand Rapids: Zondervan, 2003.

Shaeffer, Francis. *Art and the Bible.* Downers Grove Ill.: Intervarsity Press, 1973.

Snyder, James L., compiler. *Tozer on Worship and Entertainment.* Camp Hill, Pa.: Christian Publications, 1997.

Stetzer, Ed, and David Putnam. *Breaking the Missional Code.* Nashville: B & H Publishing, 2006.

Stone, Kimberlee, and Regi Stone. "We Were Made to Worship Him," from *Perspectives on Worship: Vol. I.* Nashville: Experience Worship, 2008.

Strong, James. *The New Strong's Exhaustive Concordance of the Bible.* Nashville: Thomas Nelson, 2009.

Thomas, Gary. *Sacred Pathways: Discover Your Soul's Path to God.* Grand Rapids: Zondervan, 2010.

Tozer, A.W. *The Knowledge of the Holy.* New York: HarperOne, 1961.

Van Rheenen, Gailyn. *Missions: Biblical Foundations and Contemporary Strategies.* Grand Rapids: Zondervan, 1996.

Warren, Rick. *The Purpose Driven Life.* Grand Rapids: Zondervan, 2002.

Webber, Robert. *Worship Is a Verb.* 2nd ed. Peabody, Mass.: Hendrickson Publishers, 1996.

Articles

"Top Trends of 2011: Changing Role of Christianity." No pages. Online: http://www.barna.org/faith-spirituality/543-top-trends-of-2011-changing-role-of-christianity.

Best, Harold M. "When Is Worship Worship?" No pages. Online: http://www.leaderu.com/offices/haroldbest/worship.html.

Colter, Shaayah. "Atheist shocked when church helps with bills." *Southern Baptist Texan.* 2012.

Deutschman, Alan. "Change or Die," *Fast Company.* May 2005.

Doran, George; Arthur Miller and James Cunningham. "There's a S.M.A.R.T. way to write management goals and objectives," *Management Review.* November 1981.

Greear, J.D. "Artistry, Excellence, and the Mission." No pages. Online: www.jdgreear.com/my_weblog/2010/07.

Iorg, Jeff. "Learning Outcomes and Discipleship: A Sermon on the Church at Antioch." *SBC Life.* Spring 2013.

Kauflin, Bob. "Idolatry on Sunday Mornings, Pt. 1." No pages. Online: http://www.worshipmatters.com/2005/11/29/worship-service-idolatry-on-sunday-mornings. November 29, 2005.

Leafblad, Bruce H. "Worship 101: Recovering the Priority of God." No pages. Online: http://www.ozcorners.net/worship/19-worshiparticles/30-worship-101-recovering-the-priority-of-god.

Ledbetter, Tammi Reed. "Luter sees genuine open door for ethnic groups." *Baptist Press.* June 20, 2012.

Roach, David. "Pastors Uphold Christian Exclusivity Poll Finds," *LifeWay Research.* March 2012. Online: www.lifeway.com/research.

Sells, Lisa. "Discipleship Revolution." *Mission Frontiers.* January February 2011.

Spinks, Bryan. "Worshiping the Lamb or Entertaining the Sheep," *Modern Reformation.* November December 1999, Vol. 8, No. 6.

Spurgeon, Charles. "A Sermon and a Reminiscence," *Sword and Trowel* (1873). No pages. Online: http://www.spurgeon.org/s_and_t/srmn1873.htm.

Watke, Curt. "Understanding Your Missional Culturescape: a white paper on defining 'people groups' for mission and ministry." No pages. Online: www.missionalcyclopedia.org. December 5, 2008.

Weeks, Lee. "Artist's handiwork draws others to Christ." *Baptist Press*. Feb. 17, 2003.

Willis, Avery. "Storying Going Mainstream." No pages. Online: www.navigators.org/us/view/urban/Orality/items/Storying%20Going%20Mainstream.pdf. December 15, 2005.

Hymns

Bennard, George. "The Old Rugged Cross."

Bliss, Phillip P. "Hallelujah, What a Savior."

Crosby, Fanny. "Jesus, Keep Me Near the Cross."

Crosby, Fanny. "Redeemed, How I Love to Proclaim It."

Francis of Assisi; paraphrased by William Draper and Thomas Ken. "All Creatures of Our God and King."

Francis, Samuel Trevor. "O the Deep, Deep Love of Jesus."

Gabriel, Charles H. "I Stand Amazed in the Presence."

Hall, Elvina M. "Jesus Paid It All."

Newell, William R. "At Calvary."

Newton, John. "Amazing Grace! How Sweet the Sound."

Watts, Isaac. "Alas, and Did My Savior Bleed."

Watts, Isaac. "Am I a Soldier of the Cross."

Watts, Isaac. "When I Survey the Wondrous Cross."

Wesley, Charles. "And Can It Be."

Work, John Jr., and John Work. "Were You There."